C.R.A.F.T YOUR AI MASTERMIND

Master the Art of Building and Leading with Artificial Intelligece

RAJ VARMA

BlueRose ONE.com
Stories Matter
NewDelhi • London

BLUEROSE PUBLISHERS
India | U.K.

BlueRose ONE.com
Stories Matter
New Delhi • London

For permissions requests or inquiries regarding this publication,
please contact:

BLUEROSE PUBLISHERS
www.BlueRoseONE.com
info@bluerosepublishers.com
+91 8882 898 898
+4407342408967

ISBN: 978-93-7310-951-0

Cover design: Yash Singhal
Typesetting: Namrata Saini

First Edition: December 2025

Dedication

To my family,

The original network of support,
The processors of my dreams,
And the power source of my inspiration.

You've been my constant connection,
Upgrading me with your love,
Debugging my doubts,
And coding resilience into my journey.

This book is for you,
With gratitude beyond measure.

– Raj Varma

Introduction

What this book is—and isn't

It is a blueprint for deploying AI agents as part of a broader operating system. You'll find playbooks for five core domains where agents already deliver measurable ROI—Communication, Research, Analytics, Functional operations, and Technical Work. You'll also find the scaffolding that turns prototypes into production: governance, observability, memory hygiene, and human-in-the-loop controls.

It is not a "prompt magic" compendium, nor a promise that agents can (or should) replace judgment, creativity, or accountability. Agents extend reach and reduce latency; they don't absolve leaders from leading. Where the work touches people—customers, employees, patients—disclosure, consent, and dignity are non-negotiable.

A market larger—and nearer—than expected

Analysts and operators alike now talk in billions with a straight face. The agent economy—spanning infrastructure, models, orchestration platforms, and vertical solutions—has already crossed into hundreds of billions in enterprise value and is throwing off real revenue. Compute providers, model vendors, and managed-agent platforms expect tens of billions in the near term as companies re-platform workflows. If that sounds abstract, translate it into the microeconomics of a single team: cycle times shrink from months to days; queues disappear; backlogs turn into simulations; throughput becomes elastic; and the cost of an iteration falls toward zero. That is where value is created.

Speed is not a vanity metric. It is a learning rate. When you shorten time-to-insight and time-to-iteration, you make better decisions sooner. Over a year, that compounding advantage overwhelms incremental efficiency. This is why I describe speed as a strategy, not a side effect.

How to read this book

- If you're an executive: Start with the outcomes. Use the rollout plan to pick three processes, cap blast radius, set evals, and measure cost per task, exception rate, and satisfaction. Insist on governance from day one. Celebrate wins, not demos.
- If you're a builder: Live in the stack chapters and CRAFT playbooks. Instrument everything. Constrain permissions. Treat prompts as code, data access as a privilege, and memory as a product. Build the escape hatches before you need them.
- If you're a team lead or individual contributor: Focus on augmentation. Identify the 30% of your work that is repeatable and high-volume; the 50% that is judgment-heavy but can be accelerated; and the 20% you want to expand because it grows your career. Use agents to reclaim time and reinvest it in relationships, analysis, and storytelling.
- If you're a policymaker or risk leader: The governance section is yours. Agents need identity, policy, auditability, and kill switches. Build model risk management that is proportionate to context: stricter for financial decisions than for internal drafts. Create clear disclosure norms.

The C.R.A.F.T. lens

The heart of the book is a simple mnemonic—C.R.A.F.T.—that reflects where agents create reliable value today:

- Communication: outreach, support, success, vendor management.
- Research: literature reviews, competitive intel, discovery.
- Analytics: querying, forecasting, scenario planning.

- Functional: finance, HR, operations, compliance workflows.
- Technical: DevOps, QA, security, data engineering.

I chose these five because they share four properties: repeatable patterns, dense and accessible data, clear tool adjacencies, and measurable outcomes. In each domain, you'll find the same spine—perceive, plan, act, reflect—implemented with different tools, constraints, and KPIs.

Principles that guide the book

- Design for outcomes: Begin with a business metric, not a model. Tie agent KPIs to throughput, error rate, time-to-resolution, revenue, or risk reduction.
- Safety by design: Least privilege, explicit approvals, immutable logs, and fast rollbacks. Assume failure modes. Shrink the blast radius.
- Memory hygiene: Retrieval beats recall. Track provenance. Require citations where stakes are high. Decay or version memories to avoid drift.
- Human advantage: Double down on what compounds with people—trust, empathy, narrative, critical thinking. Agents widen your aperture; humans decide what matters.
- Continuous evals: Unit tests for prompts, integration tests for workflows, shadow runs before go-live, and weekly post-incident reviews. Make improvement a habit, not a project.

What changes for jobs

Work will unbundle into smaller, observable units. Roles will be redesigned around competencies and decisions, not just tasks. New roles emerge—agent wranglers, model risk managers, data product owners, safety stewards—while classic roles absorb agent orchestration as a native skill. Many jobs won't vanish; they'll tilt. The uncomfortable truth is that some will compress. The opportunity is that new throughput and new services appear when cycle times collapse. Leaders owe their teams clarity, reskilling pathways, and ethical guardrails—not platitudes.

What changes for organizations

- Strategy: Competing on learning rate—how quickly a company can test, decide, and deploy—becomes the moat. Proprietary workflows and trusted brands matter as much as proprietary data.
- Economics: Cost shifts from headcount to compute and data products. Throughput per dollar becomes a board metric. Outcome-based pricing gains ground.
- Operating model: From projects to products; from static SOPs to living playbooks; from siloed tools to orchestrated systems. Observability, not heroics, underwrites reliability.
- Governance: Treat agents as first-class identities with roles, permissions, and accountability. Build red-team exercises and incident response for agent failures.

Ethics without euphemisms

Progress without principle erodes trust. This book is explicit about ethical baselines:

- Transparency: Disclose when an agent is acting, especially in customer or employee-facing contexts where decisions have consequences.
- Consent: Give people meaningful choice where feasible, particularly in sensitive domains.
- Fairness: Test for bias and run counterfactuals. Measure impact across groups, not averages.
- Privacy: Practice minimization, retention limits, and deletion workflows. Access is a privilege, not a default.

- Environmental impact: Right-size models, schedule compute smartly, and measure energy cost. Efficiency is stewardship.

What to expect—and what not to

You'll find case vignettes grounded in lived deployments, not simulated perfection. You'll get templates for evals, governance, and rollout plans you can copy into your own environment. You won't find claims that agents are magic or that they remove the need for expertise. Expertise becomes more valuable when the busywork recedes; it guides which questions to ask, which trade-offs to make, and which risks to tolerate.

A personal note on courage and care

Adopting agents at scale requires two forms of courage: the courage to try small, fast, and public; and the courage to slow down where stakes demand it. Celebrate speed where learning is cheap. Insist on care where harm is possible. The art is knowing the difference, and the discipline is building systems that enforce it.

I hope this book helps you make sense of the noise, pick the right starting points, and build momentum with integrity. If you are a leader, may it help you create time for your teams to do their best work. If you are a builder, may it give you the scaffolding to ship safely. If you are a worker navigating change, may it offer a path to turn uncertainty into agency.

The invisible workforce has arrived. Our task is to put it to work wisely—so we can spend more of our finite human time on judgment, relationships, and the kind of progress that endures.

Raj Varma

Founder, CXO Inc

Contents

Introduction: The Dawn of a New Era **1**

Part I: A New Industrial Revolution of Software **9**

Chapter 1: The $236 Billion Invisible Workforce 14

Chapter 2: The Physics of Speed: Why Agents Win 19

Chapter 3: What Is an AI Agent? From Prompts to Autonomy 32

Chapter 4: The CRAFT Framework: Communication, Research, Analytics, Functional, Technical 44

Part II: AI's Societal Impact **69**

Chapter 5: Explainable AI (XAI) - Opening the Black Box 76

Chapter 6: The Bias Amplification Loop 82

Chapter 7: Cognitive and Informational Challenges in the Age of AI 88

Chapter 8: Future Directions - The AI Arms Race 94

Chapter 9: Adaptation and Partnership with AI 101

Part III - Impact of AI on the Global Job Market (Country-Specific Analysis) **109**

Chapter 10: United States: AI as a Job Disruptor and Creator 117

Chapter 11: China: Workforce Transformation at Scale 123

Chapter 12: India: Navigating AI in an Emerging Economy 130

Chapter 13: Europe: Ethical AI and Workforce Adaptation 137

Chapter 14: Rest of the World: Opportunities and Challenges 145

Part IV: The New Labor Market **155**

Chapter 15: Jobs That Change, Jobs That Grow 163

Chapter 16: The Agent Manager Role 173

Chapter 17: Building an Agent-Ready Organization 181

Chapter 18: Incentives, Productivity, and Measurement 189

Part V: Ethics, Governance, and Society 197

Chapter 19: Safety by Design 199

Chapter 20: Bias, Fairness, and Accountability 206

Chapter 21: Data Sovereignty and Privacy 214

Chapter 22: Environmental Costs and Efficiency 222

Chapter 23: Collective Bargains: Regulation and Standards 230

Part VI: AI in 2030 - Outlook and Predictions 239

Chapter 24: The Ubiquity of AI 245

Chapter 25: The Evolving Workforce 250

Chapter 26: AI and the Global Economy 255

Chapter 27: Ethics and Governance in 2030 260

Chapter 28: AI and the Human Experience 265

Conclusion: The Human-AI Odyssey 271

Introduction: The Dawn of a New Era

We have entered an industrial revolution that doesn't roar with smokestacks or assembly lines. It hums quietly inside laptops and clouds. The machines are not steel arms and conveyor belts; they are agents—goal-driven pieces of software that perceive, plan, act, and learn. They are not replacing apps so much as orchestrating them, threading together tools and data to deliver outcomes at the speed of intention.

In the history of human progress, few forces have reshaped the world as profoundly as industrial revolutions. From the steam engine to the microprocessor, each wave of innovation has transformed economies, societies, and the very fabric of human life. Now, in the 21st century, we find ourselves at the threshold of another revolutionary era—one driven not by physical machinery or raw materials, but by software, artificial intelligence (AI), and autonomous systems. This transformation is larger than any single technology; it is a redefinition of how we work, interact, and live.

This book, structured into six parts, explores the multifaceted impact of AI on our world, delving into its technical foundations, societal implications, and the profound changes it will bring to the global workforce and economy. It is not merely a discussion of what AI is, but also of what it means—how it will shape our future, challenge our values, and compel us to rethink the nature of humanity itself.

At the heart of this book lies a central thesis: AI is not just a technological advancement, but a paradigm shift that will redefine industries, economies, and the human experience. By 2030, AI will have moved beyond being a tool to becoming a partner—an invisible workforce of agents, models, and platforms that augment human potential while introducing new ethical, economic, and societal dynamics. This introduction aims to set the stage for that exploration, outlining the themes, questions, and frameworks that will guide the chapters ahead.

A New Industrial Revolution of Software

The first part of this book begins with the premise that AI represents a new industrial revolution—one that is software-driven rather than hardware-dependent. The $236 billion AI market, though often invisible to the average person, already powers much of modern life: from recommendation engines on social media to automated logistics systems, from financial trading algorithms to virtual assistants. These AI agents are more than just tools—they are systems capable of learning, reasoning, and acting autonomously within specified parameters.

This section unpacks the concept of AI as an "invisible workforce," exploring how the physics of speed, data processing, and decision-making enable AI to outperform humans in specific domains. It introduces the reader to the CRAFT framework (Communication, Research, Analytics, Functional, Technical)—a model for understanding the diverse roles AI plays in modern systems. By the end of this section, readers will have a clear understanding of what AI agents are, how they work, and why they are poised to dominate the next decade of innovation.

AI's Societal Impact

Part II delves into the broader societal implications of AI. The rise of AI brings not only opportunities but also significant challenges, particularly in areas like transparency, bias, and cognitive overload. The chapter on Explainable AI (XAI) emphasizes the need to "open the black box" of machine learning systems, making their decisions understandable to humans. This is crucial in sectors like healthcare, finance, and criminal justice, where opaque algorithms can have life-altering consequences.

Bias amplification is another critical topic tackled in this section. AI systems, trained on historical data, often reflect and even exacerbate societal inequalities. The "feedback loop" of bias—where flawed outputs reinforce flawed inputs—poses a fundamental ethical challenge for AI designers and policymakers. Equally important is the cognitive and informational challenge of living in an AI-saturated world, where individuals are bombarded with AI-curated content, recommendations, and decisions.

Finally, this section explores the future direction of AI in the context of geopolitics. The "AI arms race" among nations is not just a competition for technological dominance but also a struggle over values, ethics, and global influence. As AI becomes a strategic asset, the need for international collaboration and governance will grow more urgent.

Impact on the Global Job Market

Part III focuses on one of the most contentious aspects of AI: its impact on the global labor market. Country-specific analyses reveal how nations are navigating the challenges and opportunities of workforce transformation. In the United States, AI is simultaneously a disruptor and creator of jobs, reshaping industries from manufacturing to healthcare. China, with its scale and speed of adoption, is implementing AI on a massive level, transforming its workforce to align with its vision of technological leadership. India faces a unique challenge as an emerging economy striving to balance AI innovation with its large pool of low-skilled labor.

Europe, by contrast, emphasizes ethical AI and workforce adaptation, seeking to create a balance between technological progress and social responsibility. Meanwhile, the rest of the world grapples with a mix of opportunities and risks, as developing nations strive to build AI capacity while avoiding the pitfalls of digital colonialism. This section underscores the uneven distribution of AI's benefits and the need for policies that promote inclusivity and equity.

The New Labor Market

Part IV examines the changing dynamics of the labor market in a world where AI is integral to work. It identifies jobs that will change, grow, or disappear, offering insights into how individuals and organizations can prepare for this transformation. A recurring theme is the rise of hybrid roles, where humans and AI collaborate to achieve outcomes neither could accomplish alone.

One of the most intriguing roles explored in this section is the "Agent Manager"—a new profession responsible for overseeing and optimizing the performance of AI agents within an organization. This role highlights the shift from managing people to managing systems, with implications for leadership, productivity, and workplace culture.

This section also provides a roadmap for building "agent-ready" organizations, where AI is seamlessly integrated into workflows and decision-making processes. It explores how incentives, productivity, and performance measurement will evolve in an AI-driven workplace, emphasizing the need for adaptability and continuous learning.

Ethics, Governance, and Society

Ethical considerations are at the forefront of Part V, which addresses the governance challenges posed by AI. As AI systems become more autonomous and pervasive, the need for safety, fairness, and accountability will grow more pressing. This section explores frameworks for "safety by design," ensuring that AI systems are robust, reliable, and aligned with human values.

Bias, fairness, and accountability are recurring themes, as are data sovereignty and privacy. In an era where data is the lifeblood of AI, questions about who owns, controls, and benefits from data will shape the future of governance. This section also addresses the environmental costs of AI, exploring how efficiency and sustainability can be balanced with technological progress.

Finally, this part examines the role of collective action in shaping the future of AI. Regulation and standards, while often viewed as constraints on innovation, can also serve as enablers of trust and equity. By fostering collaboration among governments, businesses, and civil society, humanity can create a governance model that ensures AI serves the common good.

AI in 2030: Outlook and Predictions

The final section of the book takes a forward-looking approach, envisioning the world of 2030 as shaped by AI. It explores the ubiquity of AI, from smart cities and personalized healthcare to AI-powered education and entertainment. The evolving workforce will see new roles emerge, with humans and machines working together in unprecedented ways. Economically, AI will drive growth while also raising questions about inequality and the concentration of power.

Ethics and governance will remain critical, as society grapples with the implications of AI's autonomy and influence. Public trust in AI will hinge on transparency, accountability, and inclusivity, while the human experience itself will be redefined by AI-driven creativity, relationships, and purpose.

The Human-AI Partnership

Ultimately, this book is about the partnership between humans and AI—a relationship that will define the 21st century. AI is not a replacement for humanity but a tool to amplify our potential, solve problems, and create new possibilities. However, this partnership must be guided by wisdom, compassion, and a commitment to shared values.

The story of AI is the story of humanity: a narrative of ingenuity, ambition, and resilience. As we navigate this era of transformation, the choices we make will determine whether AI becomes a force for progress and equity or a source of division and harm. By embracing the opportunities and addressing the challenges, we can shape a future where AI enriches the human experience, creating a world that reflects the best of who we are and who we aspire to be.

This book invites you to explore this journey—its promises, its perils, and its profound implications. Together, let us imagine, question, and build the future of a world guided by the partnership of human intelligence and artificial intelligence.

Part I: A New Industrial Revolution of Software

We have entered an industrial revolution that doesn't roar with smokestacks or assembly lines. It hums quietly inside laptops and clouds. The machines are not steel arms and conveyor belts; they are agents—goal-driven pieces of software that perceive, plan, act, and learn. They are not replacing apps so much as orchestrating them, threading together tools and data to deliver outcomes at the speed of intention.

Previous revolutions mechanized muscle, then standardized processes, then digitized information. This one industrializes cognition at work. Where the first factories compressed physical distance, today's agent factories compress time: time to insight, time to decision, and time to iteration. A request that once pinballed across inboxes and queues—"qualify suppliers, forecast inventory risk, prepare customer comms, update systems of record"—now lands on an invisible workforce that gets it done before the next standup.

Why this is different

- From software as a tool to software as a teammate. Traditional applications waited for humans to click. Agents pursue goals, call APIs, draft and refine artifacts, and coordinate across systems, often without a human in the loop until it matters.
- From workflows to working systems. Instead of brittle pipelines, we see adaptive loops: perceive → plan → act → reflect. The loop is small enough to be safe, observable enough to be governed, and fast enough to be transformative.
- From dashboards to decisions. Data isn't merely displayed; it's interrogated. Agents don't just render charts; they surface anomalies, run counterfactuals, simulate scenarios, and propose actions—with citations and confidence thresholds.
- From static roles to dynamic competencies. Job descriptions stretched across tasks of varying value. Agents let us unbundle work into atomic, observable units. People move up the value stack: shaping goals, exercising judgment, stewarding trust.

The economic signature

Every industrial revolution has a signature curve. This one is the compounding curve of latency reduction. When feedback cycles shrink, learning accelerates; when learning accelerates, strategy improves; when strategy improves, advantage compounds. The return isn't merely lower cost—it's higher throughput and better timing. Ship earlier, test more, and recover faster. In aggregate, that shows up as new revenue, reduced working capital, tighter risk controls, and fewer unforced errors.

This is why the "agent economy" is not a sidecar to the tech sector; it is a re-platforming of how work happens across industries. Infrastructure vendors, model providers, orchestration platforms, and vertical solutions together form a market counted in the hundreds of billions, with tens of billions in near-term revenue tied to concrete workflows: support, finance, supply chain, clinical documentation, and software operations. The spend shifts from headcount and manual coordination to compute, data products, and managed agent services. The firms that master this shift won't just save hours; they'll create capacity for work they couldn't touch before.

What changes in the enterprise

- Operating model: From periodic projects to continuous delivery of capability. Agents are productized: versioned, observed, and governed. Playbooks replace ad hoc heroics. Incidents become teachable patterns, not war stories.
- Architecture: Identity for agents; least-privilege access to tools and data; audit trails as a default. Orchestration layers coordinate multiple agents and humans with message buses and approval hubs. Memory is designed to be episodic for tasks, semantic for facts, and collective for organizational knowledge.
- Management: Performance metrics evolve. Throughput, exception rate, approval latency, cost per task, and stakeholder

satisfaction become operator dashboards. Leaders measure learning rate as carefully as revenue.

- Culture: Curiosity becomes operational. Teams are rewarded for safe experimentation, fast postmortems, and small, constant improvements. Fear of replacement is met with clarity: what will be automated, what will be augmented, and how people will advance.

A humane frame for speed

Speed without care is chaos. Care without speed is stagnation. The promise of this revolution is to reconcile the two: move faster precisely where learning is cheap, and slow down where harm is possible. That balance requires design. We embed guardrails—approval thresholds, immutable logs, confidence-based abstention—so agents can run without running off the road. We publish disclosure norms—when an agent is acting, when a human is accountable—so trust compounds. We right-size models and schedule compute responsibly so efficiency doesn't ignore stewardship.

The human advantage

As agents take on breadth and throughput, humans double down on depth and meaning. The frontier skills are the ones that compound across contexts:

- Framing problems: asking the right question, defining the outcome, and setting constraints.
- Judgment under uncertainty: navigating trade-offs, tolerating ambiguity, and deciding when to escalate.
- Relationship building: earning and keeping trust across customers, colleagues, and partners.
- Narrative: translating complex change into stories people can act on.

- Ethics in action: choosing the line and holding it—especially when it's inconvenient.

These skills don't get automated; they get amplified by agents that clear the fog of busywork. The payoff is both practical and human: more time in conversations that matter, more cycles for creative exploration, and less cognitive tax from repetitive tasks.

How to use this part of the book

Part I sets the frame. It explains why agents are a discontinuity, not a feature update, and how to think about speed as a strategy. It introduces the C.R.A.F.T. lens—Communication, Research, Analytics, Functional, Technical—as the five domains where agent value is already reliable and measurable. It also lays out the scaffolding that makes agents production-grade: governance, observability, memory hygiene, and human-in-the-loop controls.

The rest of the book dives from principles to practice: architectures that work, playbooks by domain, rollout plans, and ethical guardrails. If you're eager to start, you can skip ahead to the 90-day plan and come back here to ground your approach. If you're shaping strategy, begin here to align on language and expectations, then move into the stack and governance chapters.

A final invitation

Treat this revolution like you would any powerful tool: with ambition and humility. Pick small, meaningful problems. Instrument everything. Share wins and failures. Invest in people even as you invest in agents. The invisible workforce is here. With clear goals, tight guardrails, and human leadership, it can make organizations not just faster, but wiser.

Chapter 1
The $236 Billion Invisible Workforce

Corporate headcounts aren't swelling, yet output is. Something counterintuitive is happening inside the modern firm: the most productive new "hires" don't show up in HR systems, don't eat lunch, and don't sleep. They are agents—goal-driven software that doesn't wait for you to click a button. You give it an outcome, it decomposes the work, calls your tools, pulls your data, and delivers results before your next standup. Around this invisible workforce, an ecosystem of chips, models, orchestration platforms, data products, security layers, and vertical solutions has coalesced into a market on the order of $236 billion. That number is less a destination than a mile marker. The road under it is a reorganization of work, the most profound since we put spreadsheets on every desk.

We used to talk about "software eating the world." That was Act I. Act II is software acting in the world. For decades, automation meant rules that snapped the moment a pixel moved. Now we have agents that can perceive state across inboxes, documents, databases, and logs; plan a sequence of steps and adjust when reality doesn't cooperate; act through APIs to draft memos, open tickets, write code, issue credits, or update systems of record; and then reflect—checking their work, citing sources, escalating when uncertain, and learning what to do next time. Think of it as compressing the distance between intention and outcome. In procurement, a request that once ping-ponged across ten calendars—"Find five suppliers who meet our ESG thresholds and can ship on our timeline"—gets executed in a weekend by a small fleet of agents that scrape disclosures, score risks with citations, schedule qualification calls, update the ERP, and hand leadership a briefing pack with options and trade-offs. The work didn't disappear; the latency did.

Treat these agents like colleagues and they start to behave that way. Give them a job description—clear objectives, constraints, and a definition of done. Give them access with accountability—credentials scoped tightly to the tasks they must perform. Give them memory, not as a black box but as something you can audit: records of what happened, facts they can rely on, norms they should follow. Give them a place to collaborate: summaries that land in your ticketing system, diffs attached to pull requests, briefs with citations and open questions. And, critically, give them governance: observability, approvals, audit trails, and a kill switch. That is how you turn a demo into a dependable contributor. That is also how you protect yourself from the very human tendency to fall in love with magic tricks that don't survive the first incident.

Follow the money and you'll see why this shift isn't a fad. The $236 billion isn't one product; it's a stack. At the bottom, compute vendors race to serve low-latency inference at bearable costs. Model providers—generalists, specialists, and tiny task-models—compete on accuracy per dollar. Orchestration layers coordinate multi-step, multi-agent work and manage memory across tasks. Data products make knowledge machine-readable and governable. Security teams are giving agents identities and policies, because "who did what, when, with which permission" matters whether the actor is carbon-based or silicon-based. On top, vertical players package agents for concrete jobs—support, accounts payable, sales outreach, supply chain, clinical documentation, DevOps—and sell not sizzle but SLAs. Revenue shows up as API usage, managed-agent subscriptions, outcome-based fees, and marketplace rev shares. Buyers are no longer paying for novelty; they are paying to shorten time-to-decision and reduce unforced errors.

Why now? Latency crossed a psychological threshold. When a machine can turn around a task in minutes that used to take days, planning cadences shift from quarterly initiatives to weekly experiments. Tooling finally gives agents hands to match their brains; the major SaaS and ERP systems expose APIs sturdy enough for serious work. Observability matured; we can trace what an agent did, what it cost, and where it erred. And the unit economics are legible. Executives can model cost per task—including inference, tool calls, storage, and human approvals—then compare it to the baseline. We are not arguing about vibes; we are arguing about numbers.

Spend a day with this invisible workforce and you start to see a pattern. In customer operations, an agent triages a queue, retrieves the relevant policy, drafts an empathetic reply, issues credits within thresholds, and routes edge cases to a human with a crisp decision memo. In finance, an accounts payable agent ingests invoices, matches POs, flags mismatches, requests corrections, and posts entries—under maker-checker controls that an auditor can love. In sales, an outreach agent builds micro-segmented lists, drafts personalized messages that reference real events, schedules follow-ups, and produces call briefs. In supply chain, a planning agent merges demand forecasts with supplier reliability, simulates a port strike or a demand spike, and surfaces actions with quantified trade-offs. In engineering, a CI triage agent clusters flaky tests, proposes fixes, opens pull requests, and pings code owners—never merging without approval. In security, a sentinel catches leaked secrets, filters the noise, and either auto-remediates within policy or opens a ticket with context. None of this is science fiction. It's just what happens when you swap out handoffs for loops and measure the results.

Inside companies, the changes are cultural as much as technical. Throughput becomes elastic. You can spin up fifty agents for a weekend push and spin them down on Monday. Queues shrink because agents don't wait for meetings; they parallelize discovery and bring you decisions, not just problems. Iterations get cheap. Running five variations of a plan no longer requires five teams. Work unbundles into observable units of competence. Roles tilt toward framing problems, setting policy, and handling edge cases. The repeatable core moves to agents. Reliability stops being a hope and becomes an engineering discipline, with approvals, confidence thresholds, and immutable logs that cap risk without capping speed.

Managing this workforce requires a different muscle. Leaders who succeed start by defining outcomes, not activities. "Reduce invoice cycle time to under four days with under two percent exceptions" beats "automate AP" every time. They set guardrails early—least-privilege access, auto-approvals for low-risk, reversible actions, mandatory human review for irreversible steps, and a kill switch they practice using. They instrument everything and run evaluations relentlessly: golden datasets, shadow runs, weekly retros that turn failures into fixes. And they communicate plainly. Tell people what will be automated, what will be augmented, how roles will evolve, and where you are investing in reskilling. Trust is a management asset; don't squander it with euphemisms.

To be clear, new workers bring new failure modes. Hallucinations aren't a myth; they are a risk to be managed. In high-stakes workflows, require provenance and citations, and give agents permission to say "I don't know" when confidence is low. Data leakage isn't a press-release problem; it's a process problem. Practice minimization and deletion; enforce row-level access; treat credentials like uranium. Compliance drift happens when policies live in binders; encode them as code and test them. Reputation is a lagging indicator; cap blast radius with pilots and gates on customer-facing actions. And don't marry a single model. Route across providers, right-size models to tasks, and mind the energy bill. Efficiency is part of stewardship.

If you want the story in miniature, consider the mid-market retailer staring down a seasonal crunch—new products, tight ESG promises, unforgiving delivery windows. Historically, merchandising took ten weeks across sourcing, diligence, onboarding, pricing, and internal comms. The team stood up a handful of agents instead: one to score suppliers against ESG thresholds with citations; one to handle outreach and scheduling across time zones; one to model landed costs under shipping and tariff scenarios; one to update the vendor master and prefill compliance forms; and one to run the portal, logs, and approvals. With human checkpoints at the right junctures, the cycle collapsed to 36 hours. Corners weren't cut; latency was. And the team didn't lose control; they gained options and presented a better-diligenced plan to the board.

So what do you do on Monday? Start small and concrete. Inventory processes and score them by volume, repeatability, data readiness, and risk. Pick three. Write a policy for each—objectives, constraints, approvals, and blast radius. Run in shadow mode and compare agent output to human work. Instrument costs and errors. Publish what you learn. Scale where the metrics support it. Keep disclosure and consent in view, especially when the work touches customers or employees.

The invisible workforce is already on the books; you just expense it differently. Manage these agents like teammates—with clear goals, tight access, real memory, and accountability. Pair speed with guardrails. Measure what matters. And keep human judgment at the center. If we do that, a $236 billion market won't just inflate a tech narrative. It will make organizations faster and, paradoxically, wiser—able to learn at the pace the world now demands while holding on to the dignity that makes the work worth doing.

Chapter 2
The Physics of Speed: Why Agents Win

If you want to understand why AI agents are not just another software fad but a competitive reset, start with speed. Not speed as adrenaline or bravado. Speed as physics—the way reduced friction changes how energy flows through a system. The firm is a machine for turning intention into outcomes. Agents remove friction at every joint: they shrink the distance between question and answer, plan and execution, signal and response. And once you see that, you see why companies that master agent-driven speed don't just do the same things faster—they learn faster than the world changes. In an era when the half-life of an advantage is measured in quarters, learning speed is the only durable advantage.

We have talked for decades about "time to market," "cycle time," "lead time," and "latency" as if they were dashboard metrics to be managed. Agents transform those metrics from management jargon into the heartbeat of the enterprise. They do this by collapsing the loops. In every workflow that matters, there's a loop: perceive, decide, act, observe, and adjust. The old enterprise stretched those loops across calendars and org charts. The agent-first enterprise pulls them tight enough that the loops hum.

Let's unpack the physics.

Latency compounds like interest.

In finance, we accept that compounding turns small differences into big divergences over time. Latency works the same way. A team that can run ten iterations in the time a competitor runs two will discover edge cases sooner, test more alternatives, and converge on a superior solution—not just once, but habitually. Over a year, that difference stops being marginal and becomes structural.

Consider product development. In a traditional setup, writing a spec, gathering data, validating a market, building a prototype, testing, and iterating might mean weeks between each step because every handoff is a small tax: schedule a meeting, align stakeholders, extract data, prepare a deck, wait for feedback, rinse, repeat. Agents collapse those handoffs. A research agent assembles literature and competitor scans overnight with proper citations. An analytics agent queries the warehouse, runs cohort cuts and sensitivity analyses, and returns not just charts but hypotheses with confidence intervals. A technical agent scaffolds prototypes, integrates with APIs, and auto-generates test suites. A communication agent drafts stakeholder updates tailored to each audience. The human team still decides—but the loop time shrinks from weeks to days or even hours. Do that for five loops and you're not just faster; you've explored a larger solution space. Compounding kicks in.

The same physics shows up in back-office work, where speed creates working capital. If an accounts receivable agent reduces invoicing delay from five days to one, accelerates dispute resolution with policy-cited replies, and nudges late payers with tailored outreach, cash comes in sooner. The firm might shave days off the cash conversion cycle without a single discount. That liquidity can fund a marketing push, a hiring plan, or inventory. Speed isn't a vanity metric; it frees oxygen in the system.

Queues are where value goes to die

Organizations are full of queues—tickets in support, invoices in AP, candidates in recruiting, tasks in engineering, purchase orders in procurement, approvals in compliance. Queues are entropy. Work waits not because it's hard but because a scarce resource—attention, time, an expert—is locked up elsewhere. We've tolerated queues by telling ourselves that batching is efficient and prioritization is leadership. Agents tear up that story.

Agent speed isn't just that they "work fast." It's that they don't wait for appointments. They parallelize. They anticipate. They never forget. When 200 tickets land overnight, a support agent classifies them, retrieves the right policy passages, drafts replies with the right tone and legal language, proposes credits within thresholds, and packages the 10 percent that need human judgment into crisp memos with the minimum set of decisions required. The queue doesn't vanish, but its toxic half-life shrinks. Customer sentiment, which decays logarithmically with wait time, stabilizes. Escalations drop because early resolution keeps issues small.

And when you make a habit of killing queues, you change behavior. Sales reps stop hoarding backlogged tasks because they believe the system will help them move quickly. Engineers merge small PRs because CI triage will sort flakes and environmental issues in minutes. Finance stops stockpiling invoices for end-of-week runs because the AP agent handles them continuously with maker-checker controls. Speed begets smoothness; smoothness begets more speed.

The three times that rule your business

Every company lives under the tyranny of three clocks:

- Time-to-insight: How long from question to credible answer.
- Time-to-decision: How long from answer to committed choice.
- Time-to-impact: How long from choice to measurable outcome.

Agents compress all three. Time-to-insight collapses because agents retrieve, structure, and analyze data on demand and on repeat. Time-to-decision shrinks because agents pre-digest trade-offs, quantify risks, and propose actions—often with side-by-side scenarios and confidence levels. Time-to-impact drops because agents execute the boring bits: creating tickets, filling forms, updating systems of record, sending communications, arranging schedules.

This is not about "move fast and break things." It's about "move fast on the cheap parts; move carefully on the fragile parts." Agents are tuned to abstain when confidence is low or stakes are high and to request human approval when crossing a threshold. A good design encodes those thresholds. But the cheap parts — the data gathering, the first-draft plans, the scheduling, the logging — are where the hours go to die. When agents consume those hours, human attention reflows to the high-leverage decisions.

The geometry of iterations

Innovation is a search through a landscape — hill-climbing toward better answers while avoiding local maxima. The more steps you can take, the better your chances of finding a higher peak. Agents change not just how many steps you can take but also how widely you can explore without getting lost.

Take pricing, a domain where companies often get stuck in "set it and forget it" because re-pricing is expensive. An analytics agent can simulate dozens of pricing strategies against historical demand, price sensitivity, and competitive moves, then propose a shortlist with projected margins and churn impacts. A communication agent drafts the customer notices with different tones — plain, consultative, value-based — and an A/B plan. A functional agent updates billing systems in a controlled pilot cohort. A research agent watches forums and support tickets for early signals of backlash. With approvals encoded, you can test and roll back without chaos. The geometry shifts from one big bet a year to a series of small, instrumented bets each quarter. In a complex landscape, that is how you climb higher.

Feedback, not just speed

Speed without feedback is just spinning wheels. The agent advantage is not just faster output; it's tighter feedback loops. Every agent run can capture traces: inputs, tools called, intermediate states, outputs, approvals, and costs. Those traces become a learning system. You can run weekly evals: Which prompts underperformed? Which tools failed? Where did the agent abstain, and was that appropriate? Which human approvals took longest, and why? One edit to a retrieval rule or a policy constraint can save thousands of dollars and hours next month. When you institutionalize that practice, you get the equivalent of compound interest in quality.

A crucial piece here is observability. In old systems, failure analysis was anecdote-driven. With agents, it can be data-driven. You can label outputs as success or failure, track exception causes, and correlate them with inputs. You can establish golden datasets—canonical tasks with known good answers—and run them after every change to detect regressions. You can compare across models and choose the right one for the job based on cost, latency, and accuracy. Think of it as Six Sigma for cognition—a control chart on the thinking work.

Speed shifts the economics

There's a myth that automation's payoff is mostly cost savings. Sometimes, yes. Often, the real payoff is timing. A launch two weeks earlier can mean beating a competitor to mindshare. A forecast that updates daily can mean ordering inventory at better prices. A compliance response within 24 hours can mean a smaller fine or no sanction at all. These are not line items you can always see on a spreadsheet; they show up as revenue durability, fewer stockouts, lower working capital, and a lighter regulatory footprint.

The cost side becomes legible too. With agents, you can calculate marginal cost per task: inference time, tool calls, storage, and human approvals. You can plot where adding more compute yields diminishing returns. You can route tasks to cheaper, smaller models when complexity doesn't justify the heavyweight brain. And because you can spin agent capacity up and down, throughput becomes elastic. You buy speed when you need it; you stop buying it when you don't.

Why speed favors the prepared

Speed doesn't help if you amplify noise. If your data is a swamp, agents will paddle but you'll still sink. The firms that benefit most from agent speed do three things right.

First, they invest in data readiness. That means clean schemas, clear ownership, row-level access controls, retention policies, and metadata that tells agents what tables mean and where the PII lives. Retrieval-augmented generation (RAG) becomes reliable when your documents are versioned, chunked intelligently, and linked to provenance. Memory hygiene matters. Agents need episodic memory about what they did, semantic memory about facts they can cite, and organizational memory about norms and constraints.

Second, they design guardrails. Speed without guardrails invites regret. Define approvals for irreversible actions. Encode policy as code—a library of constraints the agent must respect. Require citations for high-stakes outputs and set confidence thresholds below which the agent abstains. Scope credentials to the minimum necessary. And keep a kill switch—the ability to halt an agent fleet by tag, domain, or risk level. Practice using it before you need it.

Third, they practice change management. The physics of speed don't suspend human psychology. People fear being replaced, judged by machines, or left behind by jargon. Leaders must narrate the change: what will be automated, what will be augmented, how people can advance, and what support they'll get. Training isn't a one-off. Create "agent wrangler" rotations. Write "How we work with agents" playbooks. Reward outcomes achieved with agents, not just effort without them.

The cultural dividend of speed

When teams see that the system responds quickly and safely, they behave differently. They write down processes because they know automation will honor them. They file crisp bug reports because the triage agent can do something with them. They escalate early because the cost of being wrong is smaller when you can roll back fast. Meetings get shorter because pre-reads are richer. Status updates become lighter because dashboards tell the story. The organization drains the swamp of performative busyness and fills it with momentum.

And something else happens: curiosity goes operational. When the cost of asking "what if?" drops near zero, more people ask it. A sales manager wonders what happens if you change the follow-up cadence by industry. A compliance lead tests whether a new disclosure reduces inquiries without hurting conversion. A product designer tries three onboarding flows for a week each. Agents make those experiments cheap. Leaders make them safe. The culture makes them normal.

Speed across the C.R.A.F.T. domains

Communication. In customer support and sales, speed is morale. A customer who waits an hour for a reply is not the same customer as one who waits a day. Agents triage, draft, and route—pulling in policy and product context. They maintain tone, honor opt-in rules, and escalate when sentiment spikes. The result is not just faster replies but steadier relationships. And because the agent logs every decision with citations, you can audit what was said and why.

Research. The speed dividend here is breadth without sloppiness. Agents can read the world overnight—industry reports, filings, forums, academic papers—summarizing with citations and pulling out the parts that matter to your context. They can run side-by-side comparisons across vendors or competitors, highlighting differences and unknowns. They can propose interview guides, synthesize transcripts, and generate coded themes. The human researcher stops drowning in PDFs and starts thinking again.

Analytics. We've spent a decade wiring dashboards that show what happened. Agents make the dashboard talk back. Ask a question in English; get an SQL query with row-level security baked in, a visualization, a set of hypotheses, and a list of next questions. Agents don't just surface a spike; they look for related anomalies, test plausible causes, and propose what to check next. Time-to-insight collapses, and because the agent produces code and lineage, analytics becomes reproducible.

Functional operations. AP/AR, HR, procurement, compliance—these are systems of rules with exceptions. The speed play is to automate the rule-following and instrument the exceptions. Agents ingest documents, validate against policy, fill forms, request corrections, and route approvals with context. Compliance isn't a separate lane; it's embedded. Cycle times shrink without eroding control. Auditors like it because logs are better than memories.

Technical work. DevOps, QA, security, and data engineering are already loops. Agents fit naturally. CI triage runs continuously, clustering failures and proposing fixes. QA agents generate tests from user stories and track flaky tests over time. Security agents scan for secrets and policy violations, down-ranking noise and auto-remediating where safe. Data agents propose schemas, catch drift, optimize costs. Speed here means higher deployment frequency, lower MTTR, and fewer Friday-night pages.

The ethics of speed

There's a reason the fastest vehicles come with the best brakes. If speed is your strategy, safety is your system. Transparency is part of safety. When an agent is the first touch in a customer interaction, disclose it. When an agent drafts a performance review input or a financial memo, record it. Consent matters in sensitive contexts; give people a way to opt for a human.

Fairness matters too. Speed can exacerbate bias if you don't measure it. Run counterfactual tests. Track outcomes by group. If an agent's outreach performs 20 percent worse with a certain segment, ask why. Fix it. Ethics isn't a press release. It's instrumentation and intervention.

Environmental impact is part of this calculus. Speed that burns megawatt-hours haphazardly isn't stewardship. Right-size models to tasks. Cache results when safe. Schedule heavy jobs for off-peak. Measure energy cost alongside latency and accuracy. It's cheaper and it's right.

The asymmetric advantage

Speed, especially learning speed, is asymmetric. If you can run safe experiments weekly and your competitor can run them quarterly, you will out-discover, out-adapt, and out-execute. You'll spot weak signals earlier: a cost curve bending, a customer segment churning, a regulatory mood shifting. You'll try five responses while they're still drafting a memo. Over time, your processes will become a proprietary asset. The way you route tasks, set thresholds, and structure memory will be hard to copy because it's built from a thousand small choices and a culture of improvement. That is an advantage with teeth.

The limits of speed—and how to respect them

Not everything should be fast. Some decisions benefit from sleeping on them, asking another expert, or hearing contrarian views. Agents should not push you into false urgency. The discipline is to tag decisions by reversibility and impact. For reversible, low-impact choices, move immediately. For irreversible, high-impact ones, slow down and widen the circle. Encode this into the system: risk tiers that route to different workflows, with different approval gates and audit requirements. Let the agents fly on Tier 1. Put speed bumps on Tier 3.

There's also cognitive speed vs. social speed. You can generate a new plan in an hour, but your partners and regulators might need a week to process it. Build alignment time into your physics. Use communication agents to brief stakeholders early, with clarity and options. Speed that ignores people is a boomerang.

A tale of two launches

To make this concrete, imagine two consumer fintech companies planning a new savings product. Company A runs the classic playbook: a month of research, a month of modeling, a month of compliance review, a month of engineering, two weeks of pilot, launch. Company B runs an agent-augmented playbook.

Week 1 at Company B: A research agent compiles market scans, competitor filings, and customer reviews with citations by Tuesday. An analytics agent segments the existing customer base, projects uptake under price points, and simulates cannibalization. A compliance agent drafts a checklist against relevant regs and past enforcement actions. A technical agent scaffolds the onboarding flow and integrates with the core banking API. A communication agent drafts emails for five customer segments. By Friday, the leadership team reviews a memo with three scenarios, risks, and a pilot plan.

Week 2: A pilot goes live to 5% of the base. Agents monitor support tickets and social chatter, flagging new concerns. The analytics agent runs daily updates. The compliance agent checks disclosures against the checklist. The technical agent rolls small fixes. By the end of the week, B either expands or adjusts. Company A is still in research, with smart people doing careful work. They are not lazy; they are living with more friction.

By Week 4, Company B has either launched broadly or decided not to—having burned a tiny fraction of the time and money A has. If the product is a hit, B has a four-week lead in a category where lead becomes brand. If it's a miss, B has four weeks of learning and can pivot resources to the next bet. A is still smart. B is fast and informed. Over a year, that is the difference between playing offense and playing catch-up.

Design patterns that make speed safe

A few patterns show up in teams that harness speed without getting burned.

Planner-Executor-Reflector. Split the agent mind into roles. The Planner translates the goal into a step-by-step plan with milestones and checks. The Executor calls tools and writes to systems. The Reflector audits outputs against the goal and policy, adding citations or triggering approvals. The separation reduces errors and creates clean logs.

Confidence-gated actions. Agents estimate confidence and abstain below a threshold, providing a summary and request for help. Thresholds vary by task: higher for customer communications, lower for internal drafts. Confidence is a function of retrieval quality, tool reliability, and past performance on similar tasks.

Canary and rollback. Before a batch operation, agents run a small canary set and compare outputs to golden expectations. If drift appears, they halt and alert. All writes are versioned; rollbacks are scripted. Nothing is "just push it and pray."

Policy-as-code. Legal and compliance rules live as machine-readable constraints, tested like any other code. Agents call the policy engine as a tool. When a policy changes, tests run and agents adapt. This avoids the slow bleed of "tribal knowledge" drift.-in-the-loop gates. The maker-checker pattern remains a friend: agent proposes, human approves. But it's scoped to risk and reversed when safe: auto-approve low-risk, reversible actions; require approval for high-risk or irreversible ones. Approvers get concise diffs and rationales, not novels.

The strategic narrative

Every transformation needs a story people can live inside. "We are becoming an agent-first company" is not adequate. Try this: "We are becoming a company that learns faster than the world changes, by giving our people an invisible workforce for the busywork and better instruments for judgment. We will move fast where learning is cheap and slow where harm is possible. We will be transparent about what's changing and invest in your growth."

Then back it with actions. Publish a roadmap of processes you'll tackle, with dates. Share metrics—cycle time reductions, exception rates, satisfaction scores. Spotlight teams that used agents to create value and teams that called a halt when something felt off. Celebrate both. The message is that speed serves judgment, not the other way around.

The geopolitical footnote

If you zoom out, speed is not just a firm-level phenomenon. Nations compete on learning speed too. The countries that build talent, compute, data governance, and energy to support agent ecosystems will see productivity gains earlier and more broadly. They will also face the social negotiation sooner: how to distribute the gains, how to retrain workers, how to regulate without freezing innovation. Here, too, the physics apply. The feedback loops between policy and practice need to tighten. Regulatory sandboxes, outcome-based oversight, and clear disclosure norms are the public-sector equivalents of canaries and rollbacks. Move fast where learning is cheap; move carefully where harm is large. Democracies can be fast if they build trust in the process.

What to measure if speed is the strategy

If you're serious about speed, put it on the scoreboard. Track:

- Time-to-insight: median hours from question to answer (with provenance).
- Time-to-decision: median hours from answer to committed choice (with approver).
- Time-to-impact: median days from choice to measurable result (with confidence).
- Iteration rate: cycles per month per key workflow.

- Exception rate: percent of tasks requiring human intervention, by risk tier.
- Approval latency: hours from agent proposal to human decision.
- Cost per task: dollars in compute, tools, and human time.
- Satisfaction: internal (teams) and external (customers).

Make these visible. When they move in the right direction, tell the story. When they spike, do a postmortem and share the fix. Speed is an organizational habit; habits need feedback to stick.

A closing image

When I think about agent speed, I picture a city that fixed its street grid. The buildings are the same. The people are the same. But the intersections flow. Lights are sequenced, lanes are optimized, buses have signal priority, and bikes have lanes. You still stop at red lights. You still pull over for ambulances. But you get where you're going with fewer stalls, fewer horns, less exhaust, and more sanity. Agents don't give you a new city. They give you a city that moves.

That, ultimately, is why agents win. They respect the physics of work. They turn intention into outcome with less friction, fewer queues, and tighter loops. They feed on feedback instead of feelings. They make organizations both faster and calmer—because when you trust your system to move, you can focus on where you're going, not whether your wheels will fall off. And in a world where the terrain shifts underfoot, that is the only speed that matters: the speed at which you can learn, decide, and adjust without losing your balance or your soul.

Chapter 3
What Is an AI Agent? From Prompts to Autonomy

If the 2010s were about teaching machines to finish our sentences, the 2020s are about teaching them to finish our jobs—safely. That's the leap from prompts to autonomy. Yesterday you said, "Summarize this report." Tomorrow you'll say, "Close the books, flag anomalies above our thresholds, update the ledger, and brief me at 5 p.m.—with citations." We call the new worker an AI agent. The term is everywhere and dangerously elastic. Let's pin it down in a way your CFO, your GC, and your frontline team can live with.

An AI agent is software that accepts a goal, perceives the relevant context, plans a sequence of steps, uses tools to act in the world, evaluates what happened against the goal and policy, and adapts. It doesn't just answer—it does. It doesn't just predict—it performs. And, if you design it right, it knows when to slow down, escalate, or say, "I don't know."

From answers to actions

Prompts felt magical because they turned language into a universal remote. "Give me a paragraph." "Write an SQL query." "Draft a letter." The output was text on a page, ideas in a box. Agents move from the page to the pipeline. They change databases, open tickets, issue credits, book freight, file forms, schedule meetings, and ping your lawyer when a clause crosses the line. They can do that because they don't live in a single turn with a single prompt. They live in a loop: perceive, plan, act, reflect.

Perceive means the agent reads the room: the order status, the customer's history, the policy version in force, the permissions it holds. Plan means it decomposes your goal into steps and checks, with a definition of done. Act means it calls tools – APIs, apps, scripts – to change the world. Reflect means it checks its work against policy and goals, decides whether to retry, escalate, or ask for help, and updates memory. That loop, running under guardrails, is the difference between a party trick and a productive colleague.

The anatomy of a responsible agent

If you're going to invite agents into the enterprise, give them organs, not just vibes.

Perception. The agent needs to pull in the right facts at the right time. That usually means retrieval—fetching policy passages, customer entitlements, past tickets, the latest product spec, or the relevant table from your warehouse. It also means identity. Who's asking? On whose behalf? What rights does the agent have this minute? Perception is not a Google search; it's context with provenance.

Planning. Free-form cleverness is fun until it hits payroll. Good agents plan with templates and constraints. They turn "process this invoice" into a map: ingest → extract → match to PO → validate thresholds → propose entry → request approval if variance > X → post → archive. Plans have milestones, checks, and error paths. They predict cost and time. If the estimate blows the budget, the agent proposes a cheaper path or asks you to raise the cap. Planning is a data structure you can inspect, not an inner monologue you can't.

Action. This is where the rubber hits your systems. Tools are the agent's hands: billing APIs, ERPs, CRMs, HRIS, CI/CD, schedulers, email, chat, calendars, e-signature, OCR, translation, headless browsers, policy engines. Tool calls are typed, validated, and logged. Inputs are sanitized; outputs are parsed. Side effects are idempotent and reversible. Action without safety is where sunrise demos go to sunset headlines.

Reflection. Every step should end with a question: Did this move us closer to the goal within policy? Do we retry, back off, escalate, or ask for approval? Reflection uses tests, schemas, secondary "critic" models that check tone, compliance, and correctness, and confidence estimates that gate actions. Reflection is how you earn trust.

Memory. Agents need memory the way pilots need instruments. There's episodic memory (what happened on this run), semantic memory (facts and procedures with sources), and organizational memory (preferences, tone, "how we write incident reports here"). Memory creates audit trails and avoids Groundhog Day. It also needs hygiene: versioning, decay, human curation. Bad memory is worse than no memory.

Wrap the whole organism in governance: identity, permissions, logging, approvals, and a kill switch. If you can't answer "who did what, when, with which permission, and why?" you don't have an enterprise agent; you have a liability with a personality.

A spectrum: from assistive to autonomous

Not every use case needs a Formula One car. Sometimes you want a bike with good brakes.

Stateless assistants. One-and-done helpers: "Draft an email based on this policy," "Summarize this call," "Generate an SQL query with row-level security." Useful, low risk, no persistence. A great on-ramp.

Task agents. Multi-step, bounded-scope workers: "Ingest this invoice, match to PO, flag mismatches, request corrections, propose entry." They carry state, call tools, produce logs. Think AP/AR, onboarding, enrichment, QA triage.

Conversational agents with memory. They maintain sessions, remember preferences, track unresolved items, and continue work over multiple interactions. Great for support and success. Risk: drift. Antidote: memory hygiene and policy engines.

Orchestrators. A conductor coordinates specialists—researcher, analyst, writer, tester—merges outputs, enforces policy. Useful when work spans tools and skills. Complexity rises; so does the need for observability.

Semi-autonomous operators. Event- or schedule-driven agents that act within thresholds: auto-renew certificates, rotate keys, nudge late payers, reorder supplies inside caps, file low-risk compliance reports. Humans approve above thresholds.

Autonomous-with-oversight. The frontier: agents that design plans, allocate small budgets, coordinate others, and adapt to surprises—under risk-based gates. Think supply planning, campaign management, incident response. Autonomy here means "autonomy within constraints," not sovereignty.

If you hear "fully autonomous," translate to "let's talk about risk tiers."

Tools: giving agents hands

Brains without hands write nice prose and go home. Hands change outcomes.

System connectors. CRUD on your core systems: Salesforce, SAP, Oracle, Workday, ServiceNow, Stripe, NetSuite, Snowflake, Databricks, AWS/GCP/Azure. Typed clients, rate limits, retries, health checks.

Data tools. SQL engines, vector stores, feature stores, BI APIs. Agents generate queries with security baked in, produce reproducible notebooks, and write back with lineage.

Communications. Email, chat, calendar, VOIP. Templates with tone and legal constraints. Consent respected. Logs by default.

Web automation. Headless browsing that honors robots.txt and rate limits. DOM-aware selectors rather than brittle x,y clicks. Captchas handled via approved services.

DevOps/SecOps, CI/CD, issue trackers, scanners, key managers, container orchestrators. Agents open PRs with diffs, annotate vulnerabilities, rotate secrets, roll back safely.

Utilities. OCR, translation, PDF/Doc parsers, e-signature, maps, tax and currency calculators.

Policy engine. Not a nice-to-have. A must. Encode legal, compliance, and business rules as a service. Agents call it. It returns allow/deny with reasons. When policy changes, tests run, agents adapt.

Every tool runs under least-privilege credentials scoped to the agent's role. Every call is logged with inputs, outputs, latency, cost. That's not bureaucracy. That's brakes.

Memory: retrieve, don't hallucinates conflate memory and imagination. Agents shouldn't. Treat memory like a product.

Episodic. The trace: inputs, intermediate states, tool calls, outputs, approvals, costs. Gold for audits and improvement.

Semantic. Facts the agent can cite—policies, procedures, specs, entitlements, regulatory definitions—stored in versioned corpora. Retrieval via embeddings or keywords with metadata filters. Attach provenance.

Organizational. Preferences and norms: tone, definitions of "done," style guides, "what a good RCA looks like here." Curate; don't ossify; version aggressively.

Learning. Promote repeated patterns to templates, tools, or policies. Don't just hope the agent "gets better." Make the improvement explicit and reviewable.

Maxim: retrieve or abstain. If retrieval quality is low, confidence is low. Below threshold, the agent pauses and asks for help.

Planning that survives daylight

Chain-of-thought is charming. Chain-of-proof gets past your auditor.

Templates. Encode common plans with placeholders and thresholds. Prevent creative detours where you don't want them.

Decomposition. Break goals into subgoals with inputs, tools, success predicates, and error paths. Evaluate independently.

Milestones and checks. Validate schemas, compare against thresholds, call policy before writes. Plans are gates, not vibes.

Resource estimates. Predict time and cost. If over budget, propose a cheaper plan or request an exception.

Parallelism. Run independent steps concurrently within rate and tool limits. Save time where risk is low.

Replanning. When reality bites—missing data, changed conditions—update the plan and explain the change. No silent improvisation.

Reflection that earns trust

Critics. Separate models or rules audit outputs for correctness, tone, and compliance. For code, tests. For data, constraints. For text, classifiers for PII, bias, and legal landmines.

Confidence. Estimate based on retrieval quality, tool reliability, model agreement, and history on similar tasks. Below threshold, abstain.

Human-in-the-loop. Maker-checker with respect for attention: what changed, why it's in policy, diffs against current state, rollback ready.

Rollbacks. Prepare and test them. Link them in the approval. "Approve to proceed; rollback script attached."

Postmortems. When things wobble, agents draft timelines, hypotheses, and corrective actions. Humans decide, then promote lessons into artifacts.

Governance you can defend

Identity and roles. Agents are first-class identities with SSO, scoped roles, and clear owners (human teams accountable for behavior).

Secrets. Short-lived credentials, vaults, rotation, just-in-time access. No hardcoded keys. Ever.

Policy-as-code. Centralized, versioned, tested. Called like any other tool. No rules buried in prompts.

Observability. Traces, metrics (latency, success, cost), PII-safe logs, dashboards, alerts. You can't steer what you can't see.

Approvals and thresholds. Risk-based gates: auto-approve low-risk reversible actions; require humans for high-risk or irreversible ones. Practice the kill switch.

Disclosure. Tell people when agents act—customers and employees. In regulated contexts, that's not optional. Even when it is, it's good hygiene.

What agents are not

Omniscient. Without retrieval, they hallucinate. Without tools, they decorate. Without policy, they improvise. Without identity, they trespass.

A replacement for judgment. They accelerate diligence. They don't carry responsibility. Humans still set risk appetite and own outcomes.

A magic endpoint. "/doStuff" is a demo. Production agents are systems: interfaces, tools, memory, policy, people.

All or nothing. Narrow, well-governed agents beat broad, sloppy ones every day ending in "y."

Where they stumble—and how not to

Retrieval drift. Knowledge bases rot. Fix with versioning, doc hygiene, re-embedding, evals that catch staleness.

Tool brittleness. APIs change; rate limits bite. Fix with typed clients, contract tests, backoffs, health checks, adapters.

Prompt fragility. Small word changes, big behavior shifts. Fix with structured prompting, function-calling, version control, reviews.

Memory contamination. One-off incidents fossilize. Fix with decay policies, human curation, and separation between traces and promoted knowledge.

Over-autonomy. No thresholds, no approvals. Fix with risk tiers, confidence gates, staged rollouts: shadow → canary → cohort → broad.

Cost blowouts. Unbounded loops, heavyweight models for lightweight tasks, duplicate retrievals. Fix with budgets per run, token/cycle limits, model routing, caching, cost alerts.

Ethics lapses. Undisclosed agent use, biased outputs, privacy leaks. Fix with disclosure norms, bias testing, minimization, deletion workflows, and incident playbooks.

How to test agents like adults

Unit tests. Prompts, tools, and parsers with edge cases.

Golden tasks. Canonical scenarios with known-good outputs. Run before and after changes.

Shadow runs. Agents work alongside humans without acting. Compare, label, tune.

Load and chaos. Volume, noise, tool outages. Watch degradation.

Human evals. Double-blind ratings with rubrics for tone, clarity, usefulness. Measure inter-rater reliability.

Longitudinal metrics. Success rate, exception rate, approval latency, rollback frequency, cost per task, satisfaction.

Post-incident reviews. Root cause, corrective actions, test updates, policy updates. Publish the learning.

Design patterns that travel well

Planner–Executor–Reflector. Separation of concerns for clarity, safety, and logs.

Toolformer discipline. Teach when to call which tool via schemas and examples. Keep tools simple and reliable.

Critic on the shoulder. A specialized checker audits outputs; escalate on disagreement.

Confidence-gated routing. Simple tasks to small models; complex or low-confidence tasks to big ones. Always have an abstain path.

Canary-first. Sample before batch writes; halt on drift.

Policy engine as a tool. Don't hide rules in prompts. Ask the policy service.

Memory lanes. Ephemeral session notes, persistent facts with provenance, promotion only after review.

Human-friendly diffs. Approvers see what changes, why, and how to undo it. Respect attention budgets.

Where agents already earn their keep

Customer operations. They triage queues, retrieve relevant policy, draft empathetic replies, issue credits within thresholds, and escalate edge cases with crisp memos. They log the why behind each decision—with citations.

Finance. They ingest invoices, match POs, flag mismatches, request corrections, and post entries under maker–checker controls. In AR, they generate dunning schedules tailored to history and coordinate payment plans.

Sales and marketing. They build micro-segmented lists, draft personalized outreach, schedule follow-ups, prep call briefs, and monitor response. In marketing ops, they QA campaign workflows, enforce UTM discipline, reconcile spend.

Supply chain. They merge demand forecasts with supplier reliability, propose reorder points, simulate shocks, and surface actions with quantified trade-offs. They issue POs within caps and maintain supplier scorecards.

Engineering. They cluster flaky tests, propose fixes, open PRs with diffs, ping code owners. They generate tests from user stories, tune CI runtimes, and suggest cloud cost optimizations.

Security and compliance. They scan repos and logs, down-rank noise, auto-remediate low-risk issues, open tickets with context elsewhere. They draft regulatory responses with source links and maintain control matrices.

HR and legal. They prefill inclusive job descriptions, schedule interviews, summarize panels, draft offers within comp bands. They assemble NDAs and MSAs from templates, flag redlines outside fallback positions, route to counsel.

Healthcare and life sciences. They prep chart notes from transcripts with citations to the EHR, flag interactions for review, wrangle prior auth paperwork. In R&D, they synthesize literature and propose protocols with risk notes.

From pilot to practice

Inventory candidates. Look for volume, repeatability, accessible data, measurable outcomes. Score risk. Pick three.

Write the policy. Objectives, constraints, approvals, blast radius. Encode it. Don't bury it in a slide.

Build in shadow. Let agents run next to humans for a cycle. Compare, label, tune.

Instrument and evaluate. Traces, dashboards, golden tasks, weekly retros. Improvement becomes cadence, not drama.

Staff the role. Appoint an agent owner and a cross-functional trio: builder, operator, risk partner. Give them a backlog and cover.

Communicate. Say plainly what will be automated, what will be augmented, how roles will evolve, and what reskilling you'll fund. Disclose agent use to customers where material.

Scale deliberately. Expand scope where metrics support it. Raise autonomy when exceptions fall and trust rises. Keep the kill switch close.

A story in miniature

A regional insurer wanted to speed claims on minor auto incidents – scrapes, cracked windshields, parking-lot bumps. Historically, cycle time averaged 14 days: intake, documentation, estimate, policy check, payment, close. They set up a small team of agents under tight guardrails.

Perception pulled in photos, police reports, telematics, and the policy on file. Planning ran a template: verify coverage → classify severity → request missing items → estimate cost from the image library → check thresholds → propose payout. Action called tools: image models, policy engine, payment rails, email. Reflection checked for anomalies, compared to golden cases, and abstained when confidence fell. Memory logged every step, source, and decision.

Humans approved payouts above a threshold and every abstention. Cycle time dropped to 48 hours for the majority of cases, with higher satisfaction and a better audit trail. Fraud detection improved because the agents never got bored running the same 22 checks, and when something felt off, they said so. No corners cut. Just friction.

Why this matters

The leap from prompts to autonomy is not about swapping people for machines. It's about de-frictioning the distance between intention and outcome—while preserving judgment. Agents, done right, are speed with brakes. They let you move fast on the cheap parts and slow down on the fragile parts. They don't erase risk; they make it visible. They don't cheapen work; they elevate it—because the hours you used to spend on triage, transcription, and template-hunting get redeployed to choices, trade-offs, and relationships.

There's a line I keep returning to: in a world where the terrain shifts under your feet, the only sustainable advantage is learning faster than the world changes. Agents are the infrastructure for that learning. They tighten loops, shrink queues, and keep receipts. They give you an invisible workforce for the busywork and better instruments for judgment. They make "what if?" cheaper to ask and safer to try.

So, yes, let's be clear-eyed. Build guardrails. Publish disclosures. Right-size models. Track bias. Practice the kill switch. But let's also be ambitious. Teach these agents your goals, your rules, your tone. Give them hands. Give them memory. Make them accountable. If we do that, we won't just acquire machines that can finish our sentences. We'll get colleagues who can finish the shift—and hand us a clean log, a crisp memo, and a better set of options for tomorrow.

Chapter 4
The CRAFT Framework: Communication, Research, Analytics, Functional, Technical

If the last wave of digital transformation was about putting a dashboard on every desk, the next wave is about putting an invisible colleague next to every desk—and giving that colleague brakes. That's what the CRAFT framework is for. Communication, Research, Analytics, Functional, Technical. It's a simple way to organize how AI agents actually do work inside a company without turning your org chart into a science experiment.

Why CRAFT? Because most companies don't lose to competitors; they lose to friction. The right message goes out a week late. The right fact sits in a PDF no one reads. The right chart is non-reproducible. The right process dies in an exception queue. The right fix waits for the right engineer who's in the wrong meeting. CRAFT is how you hunt friction, bay by bay, with agents that move fast where learning is cheap and slow where harm is high—always with receipts.

Two premises to keep in your back pocket

- Agents are loops, not tricks. Perceive, plan, act, reflect—under policy, with memory, and a kill switch. That's the difference between a demo and a dependable teammate.
- Speed is only a blessing if feedback is tight. Every agent leaves breadcrumbs: inputs, tools called, intermediate states, outputs,

approvals, and costs. Those traces are your steering wheel and your seatbelt.

C is for Communication: where tone meets time

In business, tone is a tool and time is a tax. Communication agents cut the tax without dulling the tool. They're your first touch with customers and partners—disclosed—and your second brain for internal comms.

What they do

- Perceive who's talking, what they're entitled to, and what the history says.
- Plan the move: inform, transact, escalate.
- Act: retrieve the facts, fill the form, schedule the call, issue the credit within policy.
- Reflect: check tone and compliance, estimate confidence, escalate if unsure.
- Remember: log every step with citations and outcomes.

Where they pay

- Support triage: draft accurate, empathetic replies with policy passages, propose credits under caps, escalate edge cases with crisp memos.
- Sales outreach: build micro-segments, write personalized notes referencing real usage, schedule follow-ups, update CRM.
- Success QBRs: assemble usage, incidents, roadmaps into a deck; draft notes; set the meeting.
- Risky comms: outages, recalls, policy changes—with counsel-approved language, tone sliders, and audit trails.

Guardrails

- Disclose when the agent first touches or first drafts.

- Scope access and mask data; log who saw what, when.
- Enforce tone and legal language with a critical model.

Metrics

- First response and resolution time; CSAT by segment.
- Escalation rates and approval latency.
- Error rates (factual, policy, tone); cost per interaction.

A one-minute story

A carrier's outage days used to be chaos. A front-line agent now clusters complaints by tower, pulls incident details, drafts updates with ETA and credit policy, issues credits under a cap, and escalates the rest with memos. Waits go from hours to minutes. Refunds get consistent. Legal breathes easier.

R is for Research: breadth with provenance

The internet is infinite; your quarter isn't. Research agents read the world—and your world—so humans can decide instead of drowning.

What they do

- Perceive: define the question, map sources, retrieve with respect for robots.txt and rights.
- Plan: inclusion criteria, synthesis shape, definition of "done."
- Act: fetch, chunk, embed, dedupe, extract entities, summarize with citations.
- Reflect: score coverage and freshness, flag gaps and bias, propose follow-ups.
- Remember: versioned corpora with links; promote stable facts to a curated base.

Where they pay

- Competitive and policy watch: weekly briefs with change logs and links.
- Vendor diligence: certifications, litigation, ESG, breaches—scored with sources.
- Product discovery: interviews, tickets, reviews synthesized into themes with quotes and counts.
- Sales enablement: vertical battlecards with objections and source-backed responses.

Guardrails

- Every claim gets a link. Every link goes to a stable version.
- Label speculation as speculation. Measure and mitigate bias.

Metrics

- Coverage and freshness; citation density.
- Precision/recall on gold sets; error rates (mis-citations, hallucinations).
- Time saved to "usable brief"; downstream reuse.

A one-minute story

Procurement used to unearth ESG issues in week eight. A Research agent now compiles living dossiers on suppliers—with certifications, enforcement actions, NGO reports, and confidence scores. Surprises become trade-offs on day two.

A is for Analytics: answers with lineage

You can't steer what you can't see—or defend what you can't reproduce. Analytics agents turn questions into secure queries, charts, and narratives you can audit.

What they do

- Perceive: parse the question, map to your semantic layer, apply access rights.
- Plan: propose joins, granularity, visuals, and caveats.
- Act: generate SQL, enforce row-level security, render charts, draft narrative.
- Reflect: check against gold metrics, test for anomalies and seasonality, estimate confidence, propose next questions.
- Remember: store queries, results, and lineage in a catalog.

Where they pay

- Self-serve Q&A: minutes to answers with SQL and lineage attached.
- Root cause analysis: decompositions and counterfactuals, not finger-pointing.
- Scenarios and forecasts: ranges with assumptions and explainability.
- Experiments: sample sizes, sanity checks, readable post-reads.
- Finance ops: reconciliation across systems, with flagged mismatches and fix proposals.

Guardrails

- Lock definitions; teach the agent your metric dictionary.
- Enforce access; mask PII; cap query budgets and cache common paths.

Metrics

- Time-to-insight; accuracy vs. gold answers.
- Cost per answer; reuse of canonical queries.
- Usefulness ratings; follow-up latency.

A one-minute story

A retention dip sparked a week of arguments—until an Analytics agent decomposed by device, region, and feature exposure, isolated a confound, and produced a clear plan with SQL attached. Cooler heads, faster fix.

F is for Functional: rules, exceptions, receipts

This is the office shop floor: AP/AR, HR, procurement, compliance, legal ops. Systems of rules with exceptions—perfect territory for agents with policies encoded as code.

What they do

- Perceive: ingest docs, extract fields, validate schemas, pick the right process variant.
- Plan: thresholds, approvals, budgets for time and cost.
- Act: OCR, match to master data, compute variances, request corrections, propose entries, route approvals, post, archive.
- Reflect: check policy via the policy engine, abstain on anomalies, prep rollbacks, log reasons.
- Remember: trace everything; update master data within rules; learn exception patterns.

Where they pay

- AP: halve cycle times with maker-checker; fewer errors, cleaner audits.
- AR: smarter dunning, payment plans, faster cash.
- Procurement/onboarding: collect, validate, prefill, approve, create vendor records.
- Compliance: assemble filings with citations; route to counsel; file on time.

- Legal ops: NDAs/MSAs from templates, redline flags, routing, obligation tracking.
- HR ops: inclusive JDs, scheduling, panel summaries, offers within bands.

Guardrails

- Policy-as-code, versioned and tested. Never hide rules in prompts.
- Risk-based approvals; diffs instead of novels; data minimization and deletion.

Metrics

- Cycle time; exception and rework rates; approval latency.
- Compliance adherence; error rates; internal satisfaction.
- Fraud/anomaly lift and false positives.

A one-minute story

Prior authorization at a hospital used to be purgatory. A Functional agent assembles the request with citations, checks criteria, flags likely denials, proposes alternatives when appropriate, and tracks status. Cycle time halves, denials drop, nurses get hours back.

T is for Technical: velocity with brakes

This is the engine room—DevOps, SecOps, DataOps, QA, SRE—where agents raise the floor and keep Friday nights boring.

What they do

- Perceive: watch builds, logs, scanners, bills, schemas.
- Plan: classify issues, pick playbooks, estimate blast radius.

- Act: rerun tests, bisect, open issues, draft PRs with diffs, apply IaC in sandboxes, rotate keys, throttle jobs, page humans with context.
- Reflect: validate fixes, monitor regressions, update runbooks, label outcomes.
- Remember: timelines, RCAs, playbooks linked to changes and outcomes.

Where they pay

- CI triage: cluster failures, mark flakes, propose fixes, open PRs. Higher deploy frequency, lower MTTR.
- Test generation: from stories and bugs; track flake rates.
- Sec hygiene: scan, down-rank noise, auto-remediate low-risk, open contextual tickets.
- Cloud cost: rightsizing, reservations, drift detection, Terraform proposals with blast radius.
- Data: schema proposals, drift alerts, contract enforcement, lineage.
- Incidents: live timeline, playbooks, customer update drafts, postmortem skeletons.

Guardrails

- No merges to prod without human approval. Use canaries, flags, rollbacks.
- Keys are sacred: short-lived, vaulted, rotated, JIT access.
- Scrub PII from logs; respect residency; retain to learn, delete to protect.

Metrics

- Deployment frequency, lead time, MTTR, change failure rate.
- Security MTTD/MTTR; false positives; accepted remediations.

- Dollar savings; acceptance rate of cost proposals.
- Test coverage lift; flake rate.

A one-minute story

Friday deploys went from pizza-and-prayer to boring. A Technical agent clustered CI failures, auto-quarantined flakes, drafted fixes, and prepped postmortems. Engineers slept. Customers didn't notice. That's the point.

The cross-cutting habits that make CRAFT durable

- Policy-as-code everywhere. If a rule matters, encode it, version it, test it, and call it like a tool.
- Planner–Executor–Reflector split. The planner maps, the executor touches systems, the reflector checks and cites. Clarity is safety.
- Confidence-gated actions. Below threshold, abstain and escalate. Thresholds vary by bay and risk.
- Canary and rollback. Sample before batch writes; halt on drift; script the undo.
- Memory hygiene. Separate traces from promoted knowledge. Curate and decay. Prevent fossilized errors.
- Model routing. Small tasks to small models; heavy models only when needed. Cache. Track energy as a first-class metric alongside cost and latency.
- Disclosure and consent. Tell people when agents act. Offer a human path. Dignity is part of value creation.
- Observability as doctrine. Traces, metrics, dashboards, alerts—per agent, per workflow, per bay.
- Human-in-the-loop by design. Maker-checker where risk demands it. Approvers get diffs and rollback links, not walls of text.

- Ethics as instrumentation. Bias tests, counterfactuals, minimization, deletion workflows. Treat harms as incidents with playbooks.

Economics: how CRAFT shows up on the P&L and the board deck

- Speed: time-to-insight, time-to-decision, time-to-impact. Communication replies in minutes, not days. Research briefs appear overnight. Analytics answers in minutes with lineage. Functional halves cycle times. Technical drops MTTR.
- Quality: fewer errors, fewer exceptions, more consistency. Tone and terms stay on-brand. Synthesis is cited. Metrics are defined. Processes adhere to policy. Systems regress less.
- Cost: lower marginal cost per task (inference + tools + storage + approvals) and elastic throughput (buy speed when you need it, spin it down when you don't). Avoided costs: fewer escalations, smaller fines, less rework, less downtime.
- Time value: launches pulled forward, cash conversion improved, risk windows narrowed. That's resilience, not just savings.

Adoption: how to roll CRAFT without rolling the dice

- Map to CRAFT. Inventory workflows in each bay. Score volume, repeatability, data readiness, risk. Pick a couple per bay.
- Write the policy first. Objectives, constraints, approvals, blast radius. Encode it. If you can't write it, you're not ready to automate it.
- Build in shadow. Run agents alongside humans for a full cycle. Compare, label, tune.
- Instrument day one. Traces, dashboards, golden tasks, evals. Weekly retros in each bay.

- Staff owners. A builder, an operator, and a risk partner per bay. Give them authority and a backlog. Reward outcomes achieved with agents.
- Communicate. Plainly say what's automating, what's augmenting, how roles evolve, and what reskilling you'll fund. Disclose agent use to customers where material.
- Scale deliberately. Expand scope where metrics support it. Raise autonomy when exceptions fall and trust rises. Practice the kill switch.

A composite quarter with CRAFT

A regional retailer gears up for peak season and stands CRAFT up as a program.

- Communication launches a disclosed front-line agent for order issues. Backlogs shrink. CSAT rises. Refund language gets consistent.
- Research spins supplier dossiers with citations and confidence, making negotiations factual.
- Analytics answers self-serve questions with lineage, isolates a conversion dip, and proposes fix tests.
- Functional halves AP cycle time and files a clean compliance report with citations and zero fire drills.
- Technical quiets CI, trims cloud spend with reserved capacity buys, and turns a Saturday incident into a measured timeline and a sober postmortem.

The CFO sees cycle times fall. The COO sees queues disappear. The CISO sees cleaner logs. The GC sees filings on time and on point. The CHRO sees less burnout. No silver bullet. Just friction shaved and loops tightened.

Three fair questions

Isn't this just old automation with new lipstick? No. Old automation clicked pixels and prayed the screen wouldn't change. Agents perceive, plan, act, and reflect—grounded in your data, governed by your policy, with logs you can defend.

What about jobs? The invisible workforce doesn't erase the human workforce; it moves it up the stack. Agents take the repeatable core. People frame the problem, set the policy, handle the edge cases, build the relationships. Leaders owe teams clarity, reskilling, and dignity.

What about risk? New workers bring new failure modes. Handle them like adults: provenance, minimization, policy-as-code, confidence thresholds, staged rollouts, kill switches, model diversity, bias testing. Ethics is instrumentation, not a press release.

The closing image

If you want a picture of CRAFT in your mind, think of a port city that finally synchronized its harbor. The ships and cranes didn't change. The signals did. Pilots, tugs, customs, dockhands—everyone moves with fewer stalls, fewer horns, less exhaust. It's the same city. It just flows.

That's what CRAFT does for a company. It doesn't change who you are overnight. It changes how you move, every day. And in a world where the terrain won't sit still, movement is strategy. Build Communication, Research, Analytics, Functional, and Technical bays with agents that have hands, memory, and rules. Give them brakes. Keep receipts. Move fast on the cheap parts, slow on the fragile parts. Do that, and you won't just keep up. You'll set the pace—and you'll do it with the calm that comes from knowing your speed has a steering wheel.

Platforms, Models, and the Stack

If the 1990s were about wiring the world and the 2010s were about renting it from the cloud, the 2020s are about composing it—clicking together platforms, models, data, and guardrails so software doesn't just inform your choices; it executes them, under policy, at speed. That's the new stack. It's not a shiny chatbot. It's a supply chain for decisions and actions—a harbor with deep channels, competent pilots, trusted manifests, sturdy cranes, and radios that never go quiet.

Here's the simple truth: in a world where the terrain won't sit still, the only sustainable advantage is learning faster than the world changes—and acting on that learning with fewer errors. The stack is how you do that. Layer by layer. With receipts. With brakes.

Let's build it from the seabed up and then climb down with a buyer's checklist you can take to Monday's meeting.

Layer 0: Energy and silicon — the geology under your AI

Under every "magical" demo is an electricity bill. Under that bill is a mine, a fab, a cooling system, and a grid. The stack starts with physics.

Why it matters:

- Latency is culture. If an agent can gather context, reason, and act in seconds, meetings shrink and experiments multiply. If it spins, so do you.
- Cost curves decide what's worth automating. Pennies per task? You run it hourly. Dollars? You batch it and ration it.
- Capacity is strategy. In a supply-constrained world, reserved inference capacity is a moat. No chips, no speed.

Watch these signals:

- Memory bandwidth per dollar and energy per token. Large models are memory-bound—bandwidth is destiny.
- Inference-optimized silicon: GPUs, NPUs, smart NICs, CPUs with AI extensions. You'll route different tasks to different "brains."

- Cooling and density. Not sexy, but latency budgets and energy bills live here.

Friedman-ism in a sentence: If you don't respect geology, geology will disrespect your roadmap.

Layer 1: Models — brains with different diets

The model is the pilot guiding your ship through the channel. But there isn't "the model." There's a fleet.

Your portfolio:

- Frontier generalists: multilingual, multimodal, instruction-following powerhouses. Call them when ambiguity is high and stakes are real.
- Specialists and small models: tuned for code, math, classification, or domain jargon. Faster, cheaper, often more accurate on their groove.
- Open weights: controllable, auditable, fine-tunable—great for privacy and cost predictability, with an ops tax.
- Distilled/quantized variants: compressed to run on modest hardware or at the edge—latency where latency matters.

Principles:

- Right-size the brain. Route simple tasks to small models; save the big brain for the hairy stuff. Your wallet—and grid—will thank you.
- Ground the brain. Retrieval-augmented generation and tool use beat confident hallucination. "Cite or abstain" is a safety rail, not a slogan.
- Treat prompts like code. Version, test, lint. Use structured prompting and function calling to reduce variance.

Procurement sanity:

- Don't marry one vendor. Accuracy, latency, cost, and policy change. Keep leverage with multi-model routing.
- Ask for evals, not adjectives. Run your golden tasks. Look at latency distributions and rollback plans.
- Know your sovereignty needs. Some workloads can't leave a boundary. Plan for that now.

Friedman-ism: Bigger isn't better. Appropriate is better.

Layer 2: Orchestration — the nervous system

This is where answer engines become action systems. Orchestration turns "do X" into "here's the plan, the tools, the checks, the logs, and the rollback."

Jobs to be done:

- Planning: turn goals into steps with dependencies, budgets, milestones, and error paths. Replan when reality changes.
- Tooling: typed schemas, input validation, retries, backoff, circuit breakers, and cost/health awareness.
- Memory: episodic traces (what happened), semantic facts (what's true, with sources), organizational norms (how we do it here).
- Reflection: critics, tests, policy checks, confidence gates, abstentions, human approvals, and rollbacks ready to go.
- Multi-agent coordination: decompose, parallelize, reconcile—without deadlocks or finger-pointing.
- Observability: traces with inputs, outputs, tools, tokens, costs, and latencies. Dashboards you can steer from.

Architecture choices:

- Framework vs. fabric. Frameworks give you building blocks; fabrics give you distributed runtime, identity, and policy. You'll likely blend both.
- Determinism dial. Clamp randomness for high-stakes steps. Let creativity roam for ideation.
- Stateless edges, stateful core. Keep interactions snappy; persist traces and knowledge in governed stores.

Common face-plants:

- Tool drift (APIs change) without contract tests. Fix: adapters and typed clients.
- Prompt rot without regression evals. Fix: versioning and test harnesses.
- Runaway loops. Fix: budgets per run, step caps, watchdogs.

Friedman-ism: Orchestration is not glue—it's the air traffic control tower. If it's sloppy, everything gets loud.

Layer 3: Data and knowledge – the ground truth

If models are pilots, data is the depth chart and the buoy lights. Without trustworthy signals, you're guessing.

Foundation:

- Governed warehouses and lakes: row/column-level access, lineage, quality checks, PII tagging, retention policies.
- Document stores and vector indices: smart chunking, hybrid search (lexical + semantic), versioning, and provenance links.
- Semantic layer and metric catalog: one dictionary for "active user," "on-time," "gross churn." Agents speak your language when you actually have one.

- Feature/event stores: fresh signals for personalization and anomaly detection.

Hygiene:

- Provenance or it didn't happen. Every snippet carries a stable link or commit hash.
- Freshness budgets. Re-embed on change and on schedule. Monitor retrieval precision/recall with golden sets.

Minimization by default. Store less, mask more, delete on time. Don't put uranium (PII, secrets) in your vector store.

Friedman-ism: In the age of agents, your knowledge base is your constitution. Amend it carefully; cite it always.

Layer 4: Identity, security, and policy — the guardrails

This is the adult table: "Who did what, when, with which permission—and why?"

Non-negotiables:

- First-class agent identities: SSO, scoped roles, human owners accountable for each agent.
- Secrets management: short-lived credentials, vaults, rotation, just-in-time access. No keys in prompts. Ever.
- Policy-as-code: legal, compliance, and business rules as a service—versioned, tested, observable.
- Risk tiers and approvals: auto-approve small reversible actions; require humans for high-impact or irreversible ones. Tie to confidence gates.
- Audit and disclosure: immutable PII-safe logs; clear signals when agents act—internally and with customers.

Threats to plan for:

- Prompt injection and tool abuse. Validate inputs; sandbox outputs; default-deny external writes.
- Data exfiltration. Egress controls, DLP hooks, minimization all the way down.
- Model monoculture. Diversify. Route across providers. Watch for drift and degradations.

Friedman-ism: Security done right isn't the brake—it's the steering wheel that lets you go faster without hitting the guardrail.

Layer 5: Observability and evaluation — the instruments

Speed without instruments is bravado. Agents produce telemetry. Treat it like a product.

Instrument:

- Traces per run: inputs, retrieved snippets with sources, tool I/O, model calls (tokens, temps), decisions, approvals, outputs, costs.
- Metrics: success/exception/abstention rates, approval latency, cost per task, latency distributions, error codes.
- Evals: golden tasks, regression suites for prompts/tools, longitudinal quality, human ratings with rubrics and inter-rater reliability.

Rituals:

- Weekly quality review: top failures by impact, root cause, fix, test added. Publish the learning.
- Shadow runs: agents work alongside humans; compare, label, tune.
- Canary before cohort: sample before every batch write; halt on drift.

Friedman-ism: Show me your traces and I'll show you your future incident count.

Layer 6: Vertical applications — outcomes with SLAs

This is what people actually buy: support that resolves faster with fewer errors, AP that closes in four days with under two percent exceptions, incidents with half the MTTR. Not "AI, generally." Jobs. With receipts.

Patterns that win:

- Workflow-native: live in your CRM, ERP, HRIS, EHR, ticketing—not in a portal for portals. Write where truth lives.
- SLAs > sizzle: sell resolution time, exception rate, audit compliance, cost per ticket. Show logs and evals.
- Extensible: a safe core plus hooks for your tools, policies, and memory—without voiding the warranty.

Moats that matter:

- Data exhaust: anonymized, aggregated traces that sharpen prompts and heuristics.
- Process know-how: "how this really works here" templates, battle-tested and parameterized.
- Integration depth: typed connectors and adapters for the gnarly edges of enterprise systems.

Friedman-ism: Winners won't be "AI companies." They'll be "do-the-job" companies with AI inside and SLAs outside.

Cross-cutting glue you'll underestimate

- Eventing and scheduling: webhooks, CDC streams, buses. Agents that wait for cron are yesterday's news.
- Budgeting: per-run and per-agent cost ceilings, token/tool limits, alerts, auto-throttle.

- Content safety and red teams: toxicity, PII, bias checks in the loop; periodic adversarial tests for prompt injection and leakage.
- Localization and accessibility: multilingual prompts/retrieval, screen-reader-friendly outputs. Inclusion is a feature, not a footnote.

Economics: where the dollars hide

How it's priced:

- Consumption: tokens, tool calls, compute seconds—great for variable loads, dangerous without budgets.
- Seats/tiers: collaboration, approvals, dashboards.
- Outcomes: per ticket/invoice/claim—with quality floors and clawbacks.
- Private/sovereign deployments: VPC, customer-managed keys, on-prem models—priced like premium insurance.

Unit economics to track:

- Marginal cost per task = model tokens + tool usage + storage + human approvals.
- Quality-to-cost frontier: where a tuned small model beats a frontier model for your tasks.
- Scale curve: what happens at 10x volume—rate limits, concurrency, cache hit rates.

Moats vs. myths:

- Myth: "Owning the model is the moat." Reality: Owning the workflow, data exhaust, integration depth, and trust is stickier.
- Myth: "Open beats closed (or vice versa)." Reality: You'll run both. Design for a portfolio, not a religion.

- Myth: "One platform to rule them all." Reality: Enterprises are federations. You'll have a few spines and many apps. Make them interoperate and govern them centrally.

Reference spines you'll actually deploy

The federated enterprise spine:

- Identity/SSO and policy-as-code at the core.
- Data plane: governed warehouse + doc store + vector indices with catalogs.
- Orchestration plane: agent runtime with planning, tool registry, memory, reflection, observability.
- Model plane: router across providers/on-prem; A/B and fallback.
- Application plane: vertical agents wired into core systems.
- Control plane: traces, budgets, approvals, kill switches—one glass pane.

The edge-aware loop:

- On-device/small model for perception and quick moves.
- Event gateway to cloud for heavy reasoning or multi-system writes.
- Synced semantic cache to avoid redundant fetches.
- Policy checks at edge and core; deferred writes until central approval.
- Offline-first fallbacks with reconciliation (field service, retail, logistics).

Pitfalls that eat quarters

- Sloppy retrieval: bad chunking, no versioning, no gold sets. Outcome: convincing nonsense. Fix: own retrieval as a product.

- Tool sprawl: ad hoc wrappers, no contracts. Outcome: brittle calls. Fix: central tool registry with schemas and contract tests.
- Prompt spaghetti: unversioned prompts everywhere. Outcome: spooky regressions. Fix: prompt packages and CI evals.
- Over-autonomy: no thresholds, no approvals. Outcome: small oops becomes big oops. Fix: risk tiers, confidence gates, staged rollouts.
- Cost blowouts: heavyweight models on lightweight tasks, runaway loops. Fix: budgets, routing, caching, alerts, and an owner.
- Compliance-as-afterthought: missing logs, disclosures, residency errors. Fix: policy-as-code and disclosure by design.

KPIs for the stack itself

- Coverage: percent of target workflows on agents; percent with golden tests.
- Quality: success/exception/abstention rates; retrieval/prompt drift frequency.
- Speed: time-to-insight, time-to-decision, time-to-impact per workflow.
- Cost: marginal cost per task; model/tool cost share; cache hit rates.
- Risk: incidents by severity; MTTD/MTTR; approval latency.
- Trust: disclosure adherence; bias metrics; audit findings.
- Energy: tokens per joule; energy per task; carbon intensity if tracked.

A buyer's checklist you can use tomorrow

- Show me traces from three successful runs and one failed run. Where did it break? What did it cost?

- Run my golden tasks. Accuracy, latency, model/tool usage—under load.
- How do you encode our policies? Where do they live? How do we test changes?
- What's your kill switch story? Practice it with me.
- Can you run with my identity and data plane? What leaves my VPC? What can be sovereign?
- How do you route across models? How do we set budgets? What alerts fire and to whom?
- Show me your last postmortem. What changed because of it?

A composite day in the life of a stack

8:00 a.m. A support agent triages an overnight spike, anchors responses in policy text, issues credits under caps, escalates edge cases with memos. The orchestration layer logs every move; the policy engine signs off.

9:30 a.m. A research agent posts a brief on a competitor's pricing change—screenshots archived, citations linked, confidence noted. Product adjusts tests by lunch.

11:00 a.m. Analytics answers, "Did the weekend promo cannibalize renewals?" with a chart, SQL, lineage, and a caveat about seasonality. Finance signs off on next weekend's variant.

1:00 p.m. AP posts a batch with maker-checker. Two anomalies abstain and route to a human with diffs and rollback scripts attached.

3:00 p.m. CI wobbles. The technical agent clusters failures, quarantines flakes, drafts two PRs. An incident agent assembles a live timeline and a draft customer update. By 4:00, the fix is merged; by 5:00, the postmortem skeleton is ready.

Underneath: models routed by task; retrieval with provenance; identity and policy on every call; costs capped; energy tracked; dashboards humming. Above: teams moving with calm speed.

The closing image

When I picture platforms, models, and the stack, I don't see a startup pitch deck. I see a port city that finally synchronized its harbor. The deep-water channel is your silicon and energy. The pilots are your models. The cranes and tugs are your orchestration and tools. The manifests and customs are your data and policy. The radios and radar are your observability. And the ships – the only reason any of this exists – are your applications delivering goods on time, with the paperwork clean.

Dredge the channel, train the pilots, maintain the cranes, digitize the manifests, and keep the radios clear. Then set a schedule you can hit. You'll get fewer stalls, fewer horns, less exhaust – and more trade. That's not a new city. That's the same city, finally flowing.

Build your stack that way – humble about physics, pragmatic about trade-offs, disciplined about guardrails – and you won't just have smarter software. You'll have a smarter organization: one that can compose capabilities quickly, govern them tightly, and learn at the pace the world now demands, without losing its balance or its soul.

Part II: AI's Societal Impact

In 2018, a self-driving car operated by Uber struck and killed a pedestrian in Arizona. The tragedy, which could have been avoided by a more attentive safety driver or better algorithms, sent shockwaves through the tech world. For a moment, it forced a reckoning: AI, heralded as the technology to transform modern life, also carried risks that could endanger it. The incident wasn't just about a car—it was a cautionary tale about the far-reaching societal consequences of artificial intelligence.

Artificial intelligence is no longer a futuristic concept. It's embedded in everything from the ads we see online to the decisions about our creditworthiness, the diagnoses we receive from our doctors, and even the sentences handed down in courtrooms. While AI has the potential to revolutionize productivity, enhance healthcare, and solve some of the greatest challenges of our time, it also has the power to exacerbate inequality, disrupt labor markets, and erode trust in critical institutions.

The societal impact of AI is a dual-edged sword. On one hand, it promises unparalleled efficiency, insight, and innovation. On the other, it raises fundamental questions about ethics, fairness, and accountability. This chapter explores how AI is reshaping society, the benefits it offers, and the challenges we must navigate to ensure it serves humanity rather than divides it.

A Double-Edged Sword: The Promise and Peril of AI

Artificial intelligence holds immense promise. It can process vast amounts of data in seconds, identify patterns invisible to the human eye, and make predictions with astonishing accuracy. For instance, AI systems are revolutionizing healthcare by detecting diseases like cancer at earlier stages, often with greater precision than human doctors. In agriculture, AI-powered drones analyze crop health, helping farmers optimize yields and reduce waste. In education, personalized learning platforms adjust to students' unique needs, making education more accessible and effective.

But alongside these advancements are profound risks. AI systems are only as good as the data they're trained on—and when that data reflects human biases, the systems inherit them. In 2019, a now-infamous study revealed that facial recognition algorithms were significantly less accurate at identifying people of color, raising concerns about their use in policing and surveillance. These errors aren't just technical glitches; they have real-world consequences, disproportionately impacting marginalized communities.

The promise of AI lies in its ability to amplify human capabilities and solve problems at scale. The peril lies in its potential to perpetuate inequality, automate discrimination, and erode accountability. The challenge for society is to harness AI's benefits while mitigating its risks.

AI and the Labor Market: Disruption or Opportunity?

One of the most immediate and visible impacts of AI is its effect on jobs. Automation, powered by AI, is reshaping industries at an unprecedented pace. In manufacturing, robots equipped with machine learning algorithms are assembling cars, sorting packages, and even performing quality control. In retail, AI-driven inventory systems are reducing the need for human stock managers. And in transportation, self-driving trucks threaten to displace millions of drivers.

For workers, this wave of automation brings both anxiety and opportunity. According to a 2020 report by the World Economic Forum, 85 million jobs could be displaced by AI by 2025—but 97 million new jobs could also be created. These new roles will likely require skills in data analysis, programming, and AI oversight, shifting the demand from manual labor to cognitive labor.

Take the example of radiologists, a profession long considered immune to automation. AI systems like DeepMind's have demonstrated the ability to analyze medical images faster and more accurately than their human counterparts. While this could make radiologists more efficient, it also raises questions: Will these systems complement human expertise—or replace it?

The key to navigating AI's impact on the labor market lies in education and reskilling. Governments, corporations, and educational institutions must work together to prepare workers for the jobs of the future. Without intervention, the divide between those who benefit from AI and those who are displaced by it will only grow, exacerbating economic inequality.

Privacy in the Age of AI

Every day, billions of data points are collected about us—what we watch, where we go, and what we buy. This data fuels AI systems, enabling them to make predictions about our behavior, preferences, and decisions. But it also raises a critical question: How much privacy are we willing to sacrifice for the convenience AI offers?

Consider smart home devices like Amazon Echo or Google Nest. These systems use AI to learn your routines and preferences, adjusting the thermostat, playing your favorite music, or even reminding you about appointments. But they also collect sensitive information about your habits, conversations, and location. This data, if mishandled, can be exploited for profit—or worse, weaponized against you.

The rise of AI-powered surveillance further complicates the issue. In China, facial recognition technology combined with AI is used to monitor citizens on an unprecedented scale. Cameras track individuals' movements, and social credit systems assign scores based on behavior. While proponents argue that such systems enhance security, critics warn that they erode civil liberties and create tools for authoritarian control.

The trade-off between convenience and privacy isn't new, but AI raises the stakes. Policymakers must establish clear guidelines on data collection, storage, and usage to ensure AI systems respect individual rights. Transparency and accountability will be essential to maintaining public trust in these technologies.

Bias and Fairness: The Ethical Dilemma

AI is often perceived as objective—an impartial system driven by data rather than human intuition. But this perception is misleading. AI systems are products of the data they're trained on, and when that data reflects societal biases, the systems amplify them. This creates a dangerous feedback loop, where existing inequalities are perpetuated and even exacerbated by AI.

In 2016, a ProPublica investigation revealed that COMPAS, an AI tool used to predict recidivism in the U.S. criminal justice system, was biased against Black defendants. The system was more likely to falsely flag Black defendants as high risk, while underestimating the risk posed by white defendants. Similar biases have been found in hiring algorithms, credit scoring systems, and even healthcare tools.

Addressing bias in AI requires more than technical fixes; it demands a cultural shift in how these systems are designed and deployed. Developers must prioritize diversity in training data, test systems for disparate impacts, and include ethicists in the development process. Regulators, meanwhile, must create standards to ensure fairness and accountability in AI applications.

Trust in Institutions and Technology

As AI becomes more pervasive, it's reshaping not only individual experiences but also societal trust in institutions. In finance, algorithms determine creditworthiness and approve loans. In healthcare, they guide treatment decisions. In law enforcement, they predict crime hotspots and assess risks. While these applications can improve efficiency, they also raise profound questions about accountability and oversight.

When an AI system makes a mistake—whether it's a misdiagnosis, a wrongful arrest, or a denied insurance claim—who is responsible? The developer? The organization that deployed the system? Or the system itself? These questions highlight the urgent need for governance frameworks that define responsibility and ensure recourse for those impacted by AI decisions.

Public trust in AI also hinges on transparency. People are more likely to accept and adopt AI systems when they understand how decisions are made. Explainable AI, which provides insights into the logic behind AI predictions, is a critical step in building that trust. Without transparency, AI risks becoming a tool of exclusion rather than empowerment.

The Global Divide: Winners and Losers

AI's societal impact isn't evenly distributed. Wealthy nations and corporations are reaping the benefits of AI innovation, while poorer regions risk being left behind. The global AI race isn't just about technology—it's about power, influence, and economic advantage.

In countries like the U.S. and China, AI is driving growth in industries from e-commerce to healthcare. But in developing nations, the lack of infrastructure, expertise, and investment in AI is widening the global inequality gap. While AI-powered tools could transform agriculture, education, and healthcare in these regions, access remains limited.

This divide isn't just an economic issue; it's a moral one. Ensuring equitable access to AI's benefits will require international collaboration, investment in education and infrastructure, and policies that prioritize inclusion. AI has the potential to uplift humanity—but only if its resources and opportunities are shared.

The Future of AI in Society

Artificial intelligence is reshaping society in ways that were once the stuff of science fiction. It has the power to cure diseases, transform industries, and improve lives. But it also has the potential to deepen inequality, erode privacy, and undermine trust. The choices we make today will determine whether AI becomes a tool for empowerment or a driver of division.

The future of AI in society isn't just a technological question—it's a human one. How do we ensure that AI reflects our values rather than distorting them? How do we balance innovation with ethics, progress with fairness? These are the challenges we must confront as AI continues to evolve.

As with any transformative technology, the impact of AI will depend not on the technology itself, but on how we choose to use it. The responsibility lies with all of us—developers, policymakers, business leaders, and citizens—to shape a future where AI serves humanity, not the other way around.

Chapter 5
Explainable AI (XAI) – Opening the Black Box

In 2020, a healthcare AI system denied critical insurance claims for cancer patients, leaving families and doctors scrambling for answers. Despite the sophisticated algorithms behind the system, no one—not the developers, the administrators, or the patients—could decipher why the claims were denied. The system was a "black box," an opaque decision-making engine operating beyond human understanding. The result: frustration, mistrust, and lives left in limbo.

The story highlights a growing problem in artificial intelligence. AI systems are increasingly responsible for high-stakes decisions in healthcare, finance, criminal justice, and countless other fields. Their complexity, while a source of their power, often makes them impenetrable even to the experts who design them. This lack of transparency erodes trust, hampers accountability, and can lead to significant ethical and operational failures.

Explainable AI (XAI) is emerging as the solution to this challenge. By providing clarity on how AI systems make decisions, XAI ensures these technologies remain trustworthy, auditable, and aligned with human values. The goal is simple but ambitious: to open the black box.

The Need for Explainability

At its core, artificial intelligence relies on models—mathematical systems that analyze data, identify patterns, and make predictions. Traditional models, like linear regression or decision trees, are relatively easy to understand. Their logic is straightforward: input data goes through a transparent process to produce an output. But modern AI, particularly deep learning, is far more complex. These systems are powered by neural networks with millions or even billions of parameters interacting in ways that defy intuition. They excel at tasks like image recognition or language translation but offer little insight into how they arrive at their conclusions.

This opacity is not just an academic issue. In industries where errors can have life-altering consequences, the inability to explain decisions can be catastrophic. Consider an AI system in criminal justice that assesses the likelihood of a defendant reoffending. If the system recommends denying bail, judges and lawyers must understand the reasoning behind the decision. Was it based on relevant factors, or did the model unintentionally penalize defendants from certain demographics? Without explainability, there's no way to know—and no way to fix potential biases.

Transparency is critical, not just for accuracy, but for trust. People are more likely to adopt AI systems when they understand how they work. An opaque system might deliver impressive results, but if users can't see the logic behind it, they may resist its adoption or misuse it. Explainability bridges this gap, making AI systems not only more transparent but also more effective.

How Explainable AI Works

Explainable AI isn't a single technology but a collection of methods and tools aimed at demystifying complex models. One approach, known as post-hoc explainability, focuses on interpreting decisions after they've been made. Consider a bank using AI to assess loan applications. When the system rejects an applicant, post-hoc methods can highlight the factors behind the decision. Tools like SHAP (SHapley Additive exPlanations) and LIME (Local Interpretable Model-agnostic Explanations) break down the decision-making process, showing how much weight the system gave to factors like income, credit score, and debt-to-income ratio.

Another approach involves designing models to be inherently interpretable. Decision trees and linear regression are classic examples. These models trade complexity for clarity, making them easier for humans to understand. While they may lack the predictive power of deep learning, their simplicity often makes them more suitable for high-stakes applications where trust is paramount.

Visualization also plays a key role in explainability. In medical AI, for instance, tools like saliency maps can highlight areas of an X-ray or MRI that influenced a diagnosis. This allows doctors to see the same patterns the AI detected, fostering collaboration between human expertise and machine intelligence.

Explainability isn't limited to technical users. Some AI systems generate natural language explanations, offering textual justifications for their decisions. For example, an AI-powered recommendation system might tell a customer, "We suggested this product because customers with similar preferences also liked it." These explanations, while simple, can significantly improve user trust and engagement.

The Benefits of XAI

Explainable AI offers tangible benefits across industries. One of the most significant is trust. When users understand how AI systems work, they are more likely to rely on them. Take autonomous vehicles, for example. A self-driving car that explains its actions—"I stopped because a pedestrian entered the crosswalk"—builds confidence among passengers and regulators alike. This transparency isn't just reassuring; it's essential for widespread adoption.

Another critical benefit of XAI is its ability to detect and correct bias. AI systems are only as good as the data they are trained on, and biased data can lead to biased decisions. In one infamous case, a hiring algorithm systematically favored male candidates over equally qualified females. By using XAI tools, the company identified and addressed the underlying bias in its training data, ensuring fairer outcomes in future hiring decisions.

Regulatory compliance is another area where XAI proves invaluable. In Europe, the General Data Protection Regulation (GDPR) grants individuals the "right to explanation" when decisions are made by automated systems. Similar laws are emerging worldwide, requiring organizations to make AI systems auditable and accountable. Explainability ensures compliance with these regulations while also providing a competitive advantage: companies that prioritize transparency are more likely to earn the trust of their customers and stakeholders.

Beyond trust and compliance, XAI enhances decision-making itself. By understanding how AI systems weigh different factors, users can refine and optimize their models. In healthcare, for instance, doctors using AI-powered diagnostic tools can combine machine recommendations with their clinical judgment, leading to better patient outcomes.

Challenges and Trade-Offs

For all its promise, XAI faces significant challenges. The most obvious is the trade-off between accuracy and interpretability. Simpler models are easier to explain but may be less accurate than their complex counterparts. Deep learning systems, while powerful, often resist simplification without losing predictive quality. Organizations must balance these competing priorities, choosing the right model for the task at hand.

Another challenge is scalability. Explaining the decisions of a single AI model is one thing; explaining the behavior of a large-scale system, like Google's search engine or Amazon's recommendation engine, is far more complex. These systems involve millions of interdependent components, making comprehensive explainability a daunting task. interpretability also presents a hurdle. Even the most advanced XAI tools must present their findings in a way that non-technical users can understand. A heatmap or saliency map might make sense to a data scientist but could confuse a business executive or policymaker. Striking the right balance between technical accuracy and user comprehension is an ongoing challenge for the field.

Finally, as AI systems grow more complex, the challenge of making them explainable only deepens. Generative AI models, like those used in natural language processing, operate on a scale and sophistication that often defies easy interpretation. Yet, as these models become more embedded in daily life, the demand for explainability will only increase.

Real-World Applications

The impact of XAI is already being felt across industries. In healthcare, AI systems are helping doctors diagnose diseases with unprecedented accuracy. Explainability ensures that these systems are not only accurate but also trusted. For instance, a cancer detection system might highlight the specific features of a medical image that led to its diagnosis, allowing doctors to verify the findings.

In finance, XAI is improving transparency in areas like loan approvals and fraud detection. A bank's AI system might deny a loan application, but with explainability tools, it can show that the decision was based on income, credit score, and debt-to-income ratio. This transparency not only builds trust but also helps institutions meet regulatory requirements.

Autonomous vehicles are another area where XAI is making a difference. Self-driving cars equipped with explainability features can provide real-time insights into their decision-making processes, addressing safety concerns and fostering public confidence.

Even in criminal justice, a field fraught with ethical challenges, XAI is proving valuable. Risk assessment tools used for bail or sentencing decisions are being made more transparent, allowing judges and lawyers to understand the factors behind the system's recommendations. This level of accountability is essential for ensuring fairness and avoiding systemic bias.

The Future of Explainable AI

Explainable AI is more than a technical innovation; it is a societal imperative. As AI systems become increasingly integrated into our lives, their transparency will determine whether they are trusted or feared. Emerging trends, such as explainability in generative AI and the development of AI governance frameworks, will shape the future of this field.

The stakes are high. In a world where AI decisions affect everything from the products we buy to the healthcare we receive, explainability is not just a feature—it is a necessity. By opening the black box, XAI ensures that artificial intelligence serves humanity with fairness, accountability, and trust. In doing so, it paves the way for a future where technology and society are not at odds but in harmony.

Chapter 6
The Bias Amplification Loop

In 2014, Amazon began experimenting with an AI-powered hiring tool, designed to streamline its recruitment process by identifying top candidates. Using resumes from the past decade to train the model, the system quickly revealed a disturbing pattern: it consistently downgraded applications from women. Since the majority of resumes in the dataset came from men, the AI interpreted maleness as a proxy for higher qualifications. Amazon ultimately scrapped the tool, but the incident exposed a troubling reality: artificial intelligence doesn't just reflect human bias—it amplifies it.

This phenomenon, known as the **bias amplification loop**, is one of the most pressing societal challenges posed by AI. At its core, the issue stems from the way AI systems are trained. These models rely on vast datasets derived from human activity—data that inherently contains cultural, social, and historical biases. When AI systems process and replicate such data, they risk reinforcing and even exacerbating existing stereotypes and prejudices, creating harmful feedback cycles.

The implications of this amplification are profound. AI systems are no longer confined to low-stakes applications like recommending a movie or curating a playlist. They are dictating who gets hired, who qualifies for a loan, and even who gets released from prison. Without intervention, these systems risk locking societies into cycles of inequality, creating a future that is less fair than the past.

Breaking the bias amplification loop requires not just technical solutions, but also cultural and institutional shifts. It demands that we rethink how we design, deploy, and oversee AI systems. The stakes couldn't be higher:

in a world increasingly shaped by algorithms, the fight against bias is a fight for justice, accountability, and progress.

Understanding the Bias Amplification Loop

To grasp how AI amplifies bias, it's critical to understand how these systems are built. Machine learning models are trained on historical data, which serves as both their foundation and their fuel. For example, an AI system designed to predict who should be hired might be trained on resumes of previous employees. If the historical data reflects biases—such as a preference for male candidates or graduates from elite universities—the AI will learn and replicate those patterns.

The amplification occurs when the system isn't just passively reflecting existing biases, but actively reinforcing them. This happens in two key ways. First, AI models often prioritize patterns of success in their training data without questioning the ethical implications of those patterns. Second, because AI systems are increasingly deployed at scale, their biased decisions can ripple across entire industries, influencing future datasets and creating a feedback loop.

Consider facial recognition technology. Studies have consistently shown that these systems are less accurate at identifying people of color, particularly Black women. This isn't because AI is inherently racist—it's because the training data used to develop these systems often skews toward lighter-skinned individuals. When such systems are deployed in law enforcement, the stakes become dangerously high. Incorrect identifications can lead to wrongful arrests, perpetuating systemic inequalities and further embedding bias into the broader criminal justice system.

Case Study: Criminal Justice and COMPAS

One of the most infamous examples of the bias amplification loop is the COMPAS algorithm, a tool widely used in the United States to predict the likelihood of recidivism among defendants. Designed to assist judges in decisions about bail and sentencing, COMPAS analyzes a defendant's profile and assigns a risk score. On the surface, it seems like an objective way to reduce human bias. Yet, a 2016 investigation by ProPublica revealed that COMPAS was far from impartial.

The analysis showed that COMPAS was significantly more likely to flag Black defendants as high risk, even when they did not reoffend. Conversely, it underestimated the risk of white defendants who went on to commit new crimes. This wasn't because the developers intentionally programmed the system to discriminate—it was a byproduct of training the algorithm on biased historical data. The system perpetuated the racial disparities already present in the criminal justice system, amplifying them under the guise of objectivity.

The COMPAS controversy underscores a fundamental issue: AI systems often conceal bias behind a veneer of neutrality. Because algorithms are seen as scientific and precise, their outputs are rarely questioned. This deference to AI can have devastating consequences, particularly when these systems are deployed in high-stakes domains like criminal justice.

The Feedback Cycle in Recruitment

AI's role in hiring is another area where the bias amplification loop is alarmingly evident. Recruitment algorithms are designed to identify candidates who resemble previous successful hires. But when those past hires reflect biased decisions—whether favoring gender, race, or educational background—the AI system learns to replicate and scale those same biases.

The Amazon hiring tool debacle is a cautionary tale. The algorithm penalized resumes that included words like "women's chess club" or references to all-women colleges. By treating male-dominated resumes as the gold standard, the system reinforced gender inequality in hiring. Left unchecked, such tools risk creating a cycle where underrepresented groups are systematically excluded from opportunities, further entrenching disparities in the workplace.

Bias in Healthcare: Life and Death Decisions

The healthcare industry offers some of the most compelling examples of how the bias amplification loop can have life-or-death consequences. In 2019, a study published in *Science* revealed that an AI-powered healthcare algorithm used in hospitals was significantly less likely to refer Black patients for advanced care, even when they were just as sick as their white counterparts. The root cause? The algorithm was trained on healthcare cost data, which reflected systemic inequities in access to healthcare. Because Black patients historically spent less on healthcare due to barriers like income and insurance coverage, the algorithm interpreted this as a signal that they required less care.

This example highlights a critical issue: biased training data doesn't just skew results—it can lead to harmful and even deadly outcomes. When AI systems are deployed in critical sectors like healthcare, the cost of bias is measured in lives.

The Role of Feedback in Bias Amplification

The bias amplification loop is not a one-time event; it is a cumulative process. Every decision an AI system makes influences the environment it operates in, shaping the data that will train future systems. This creates a self-reinforcing cycle that can escalate over time.

Take predictive policing as an example. AI systems used to predict crime hotspots often rely on historical crime data. But this data is deeply influenced by existing policing practices, which tend to over-police certain neighborhoods, particularly low-income and minority communities. When the AI system recommends increased patrols in these areas, it leads to more arrests—further reinforcing the original data. The result is a feedback loop where certain communities are disproportionately targeted, while others are overlooked.

Breaking this cycle requires more than just technical fixes. It demands robust oversight, transparency, and a commitment to questioning the assumptions baked into AI systems.

Breaking the Cycle: Solutions for Bias in AI

Addressing the bias amplification loop requires a multi-faceted approach, combining technical, cultural, and regulatory strategies. The first step is improving the quality and diversity of training datasets. AI models are only as good as the data they're trained on, and ensuring that datasets reflect a wide range of perspectives and experiences is critical. For example, researchers developing facial recognition systems are now working to include more diverse datasets that better represent people of different skin tones, genders, and age groups.

Another solution lies in algorithmic design. Fairness-aware algorithms, which are specifically designed to detect and mitigate bias, are gaining traction. These systems proactively adjust for disparities in training data, ensuring that outputs are more equitable. For instance, healthcare algorithms can be programmed to account for systemic inequities in access to medical services, preventing biased recommendations.

Transparency is also key. AI systems must be explainable, allowing users to understand how decisions are made and identify potential biases. Explainable AI tools like SHAP (SHapley Additive exPlanations) and counterfactual analysis make it easier to scrutinize AI outputs and ensure accountability.

But technology alone isn't enough. Breaking the bias amplification loop also requires cultural and institutional change. Organizations deploying AI must prioritize ethical considerations, integrating diversity and inclusion into every stage of the development process. Regulators, meanwhile, must establish clear guidelines and standards to ensure AI systems are fair, accountable, and transparent.

Ethical Oversight and Accountability

The fight against bias in AI isn't just a technical challenge—it's an ethical imperative. Developers, policymakers, and society at large must grapple with difficult questions: Who is responsible when an AI system makes a biased decision? How do we ensure that AI serves the public good rather than perpetuating inequality? And what safeguards can we put in place to prevent harm?

Accountability is crucial. Developers must be held to high ethical standards, ensuring that their systems are rigorously tested for bias before deployment. Policymakers must enforce transparency requirements, mandating that AI systems are auditable and explainable. And society as a whole must demand greater oversight of the technologies shaping our lives.

The Future of AI and Bias

The bias amplification loop is a stark reminder that technology is not neutral. AI systems are products of the data, values, and decisions that shape them—and when those inputs are flawed, the outputs will be too. But the future of AI doesn't have to be defined by bias. With the right interventions, we can build systems that amplify fairness rather than inequality.

The fight against bias in AI is ultimately a fight for justice. It's about ensuring that the technologies shaping our future reflect the best of humanity, not the worst. By breaking the bias amplification loop, we can create a world where AI serves as a force for equity, accountability, and progress.

Chapter 7
Cognitive and Informational Challenges in the Age of AI

Introduction: The Hidden Costs of AI

In 2024, a junior analyst at a fast-growing consulting firm found herself tasked with developing a strategy for a major client. Instead of diving into the company's annual reports or brainstorming with her team, she turned to a generative AI tool to draft the proposal. Within minutes, the system produced a polished document, complete with insights, recommendations, and a clear roadmap. The analyst barely reviewed it before sending it to her supervisor.

The strategy was approved, but only later did the client discover glaring inaccuracies. The AI had fabricated data points, and the analyst's over-reliance on the tool had dulled her ability to spot the errors. It was a cautionary tale for the modern workplace: as AI systems grow more capable, the line between augmentation and over-dependence begins to blur.

Artificial intelligence, with its ability to automate tasks, generate insights, and optimize workflows, is undoubtedly transformative. But its growing ubiquity also carries hidden risks—particularly in how it affects our cognitive abilities and the flow of trustworthy information. When humans become overly reliant on AI tools, their critical thinking and problem-solving skills risk atrophy. At the same time, the rise of AI-generated misinformation, particularly deepfakes, is threatening our ability to discern truth from fiction, shaking the foundations of trust in media and institutions.

These cognitive and informational challenges are not inevitable. They are the byproduct of how AI is deployed and the habits we form around it. Addressing them requires a deliberate effort to rethink our relationship with technology, reframing AI as a tool that amplifies human capabilities rather than replacing them.

Cognitive Atrophy in the Age of AI

In 2021, a study published in the journal *Nature* revealed a surprising finding: people who used GPS navigation systems regularly performed worse on spatial memory tests than those who navigated independently. Relying on the technology to find directions had weakened their ability to mentally map and remember their surroundings. While this may seem like a minor inconvenience, it points to a broader issue: as AI systems take on more cognitive tasks, humans risk losing the mental sharpness that comes from doing those tasks themselves.

This phenomenon, known as **cognitive atrophy**, occurs when individuals outsource critical thinking, problem-solving, and decision-making to technology. In the workplace, AI tools are now handling tasks that once required human judgment—writing reports, analyzing data, creating designs, and even making hiring decisions. While these tools boost productivity, they also risk eroding the very skills they were meant to enhance.

The impact is particularly concerning for young professionals, who are still developing their expertise. Instead of honing their analytical abilities, they may grow accustomed to relying on AI-generated solutions. Over time, this can lead to a workforce that is highly efficient but less innovative, less adaptable, and less capable of independent thought.

The risks of cognitive atrophy extend beyond individual skills. As AI systems become central to decision-making in industries like finance, healthcare, and law, organizations may lose their ability to operate effectively if those systems fail. A recent World Economic Forum report highlighted this vulnerability, warning that over-dependence on AI could leave companies ill-prepared to navigate crises that require human ingenuity.

But cognitive atrophy is not inevitable. It is a consequence of how we use AI, and it can be mitigated by reframing our relationship with the technology. Instead of treating AI as a substitute for human effort, we must view it as a partner—a tool that augments creativity and decision-making rather than replacing them. For example, generative AI can assist a writer by suggesting ideas or refining drafts, but the writer must still shape the narrative, evaluate the content, and ensure its accuracy. This approach not only preserves cognitive skills but also leverages AI's strengths in a way that enhances human output.

The Rise of Deepfakes and the Liar's Dividend

In December 2019, a viral video appeared to show then-U.S. Speaker of the House Nancy Pelosi slurring her speech at a press conference. The video was quickly debunked as a manipulated clip, slowed down to make her appear incoherent. But by the time fact-checkers intervened, it had already been shared millions of times, fueling political outrage and deepening divisions.

This incident was a harbinger of the challenges posed by **deepfakes**—AI-generated videos, images, and audio clips that are virtually indistinguishable from reality. Unlike traditional forms of misinformation, which rely on exaggeration or selective framing, deepfakes create entirely fabricated content that can deceive even the most discerning viewers.

Deepfakes represent a new frontier in the battle over truth. By making it possible to fabricate evidence, they undermine trust in legitimate information and create what experts call the **liar's dividend**: the ability to dismiss any inconvenient fact as a forgery. In a world where "seeing is believing" is no longer reliable, the erosion of trust becomes a societal crisis.

The implications of deepfakes are far-reaching. In politics, they can be used to spread propaganda, discredit opponents, or manipulate public opinion. In business, they pose risks to reputation and security—imagine a deepfake CEO issuing a false statement that tanks a company's stock price. Even in personal contexts, deepfakes have been weaponized for harassment, with individuals' faces superimposed onto explicit content.

The rise of deepfakes has created a new arms race: while bad actors use AI to generate forgeries, researchers are developing AI tools to detect them. Companies like Microsoft and Adobe are investing in deepfake detection systems that analyze subtle inconsistencies in videos, such as unnatural blinking patterns or mismatched lighting. But detection alone is not enough. As deepfake technology becomes more sophisticated, the line between real and fake will continue to blur.

Addressing the challenge of deepfakes requires a multi-pronged approach. First, public education is essential. By fostering media literacy and teaching people how to verify information, we can create a culture of skepticism that makes it harder for misinformation to take hold. Second, social media platforms must take greater responsibility for identifying and removing deepfakes, much as they do for other forms of harmful content. Finally, policymakers must establish legal frameworks to hold creators of malicious deepfakes accountable, deterring misuse through clear consequences.

The Psychology of Overload: Navigating an AI-Driven Information Landscape

The rise of deepfakes is part of a broader crisis in the informational ecosystem. In the digital age, we are bombarded with more information than ever before, much of it curated, filtered, or generated by AI. While this abundance can be empowering, it also creates cognitive overload, making it harder to process, prioritize, and evaluate information effectively.

AI-driven algorithms, designed to maximize engagement, often exacerbate the problem. Platforms like YouTube, Facebook, and TikTok use recommendation systems to keep users scrolling, serving up content that aligns with their interests—or biases. While these algorithms can provide value, they also create echo chambers, where individuals are exposed only to information that reinforces their existing beliefs. This polarization, fueled by AI, has contributed to the erosion of shared realities, making it harder to build consensus on issues ranging from climate change to public health.

The psychological impact of this informational overload is significant. Studies have shown that cognitive fatigue, decision paralysis, and emotional burnout are common consequences of living in a hyper-connected, AI-curated world. When individuals are overwhelmed by conflicting narratives and constant stimuli, they are more likely to disengage, retreating into apathy or cynicism.

To navigate this landscape, individuals must develop new skills for critical thinking and media consumption. Fact-checking, cross-referencing sources, and seeking out diverse perspectives are essential practices for maintaining a healthy relationship with information. At the same time, platforms and policymakers must take steps to combat misinformation and reduce the spread of harmful content.

Balancing AI Convenience with Human Responsibility

Despite the challenges posed by cognitive atrophy and informational overload, AI remains a powerful tool for progress. The question is not whether we should use AI, but how we can use it responsibly. Achieving this balance requires a shift in mindset—one that prioritizes human agency and accountability.

In education, for example, AI tools can enhance learning by providing personalized feedback and adaptive curricula. But educators must ensure that students are actively engaging with the material, rather than passively consuming AI-generated answers. Similarly, in the workplace,

AI can automate repetitive tasks, freeing up time for employees to focus on creative and strategic work. But organizations must foster a culture of continuous learning, encouraging workers to develop skills that complement AI rather than relying on it entirely.

The same principle applies to the fight against deepfakes and misinformation. While technology will play a critical role in detecting and mitigating these threats, the ultimate responsibility lies with individuals, institutions, and governments. By promoting media literacy, fostering transparency, and holding bad actors accountable, we can build a society that values truth and resists manipulation.

The Future of Cognitive and Informational Challenges

The challenges of cognitive atrophy and informational overload are not unique to AI—they are part of a broader pattern of human adaptation to new technologies. Just as the printing press transformed the way people accessed and shared knowledge, AI is reshaping how we think, learn, and communicate. The difference is one of scale: AI operates at a speed and complexity that magnifies both its benefits and its risks.

The future of these challenges will depend on how we choose to adapt. If we allow ourselves to become passive consumers of AI-generated solutions and content, we risk losing the very skills that define us as humans: creativity, critical thinking, and empathy. But if we approach AI as a partner—a tool that enhances rather than replaces human effort—we can harness its potential while preserving our cognitive and informational integrity.

The stakes are high. In a world increasingly shaped by algorithms, the fight to maintain human agency, trust, and accountability is not just a technical challenge—it is a cultural and ethical one. By addressing these challenges head-on, we can ensure that AI serves as a catalyst for progress rather than a source of division.

Chapter 8
Future Directions – The AI Arms Race

Introduction: The New Battleground

In October 2017, Russian President Vladimir Putin declared, "Whoever becomes the leader in artificial intelligence will rule the world." The statement was as much a prophecy as it was a declaration of intent. Over the past decade, AI has become a new theater of geopolitical and economic competition, with nations vying for supremacy in what many have termed the **AI arms race**. This battle isn't being fought with traditional weaponry but with algorithms, data, and computing power. Its stakes are monumental, promising both immense rewards and unparalleled risks.

At the heart of this race is the tension between speed and caution. Governments, corporations, and researchers are pushing the boundaries of AI innovation, eager to gain a competitive edge. But in their pursuit of dominance, key considerations—such as safety, ethics, and transparency—are often sidelined. The result is an environment where systems are deployed before their long-term consequences are fully understood, creating vulnerabilities that could reverberate across economies, societies, and even global stability.

Yet, the future of AI need not be defined by reckless competition. There is hope for a more responsible path forward—one that prioritizes collaboration over conflict, ethics over expediency, and humanity over ambition. By supporting organizations that champion ethical AI, advocating for thoughtful regulations, and fostering international cooperation, we can ensure that AI serves as a force for good rather than a source of division.

The Stakes of the AI Arms Race

The AI arms race is not just about technological prowess. It is a battle for economic dominance, military superiority, and global influence. Nations that lead in AI will gain significant advantages in areas ranging from national security to healthcare, while those that fall behind risk being left out of the future economy.

China has been particularly aggressive in its pursuit of AI dominance. In 2017, the Chinese government unveiled a plan to become the global leader in AI by 2030, pledging billions of dollars in funding and mobilizing its tech giants, such as Tencent, Baidu, and Alibaba. The country's surveillance systems, powered by facial recognition and machine learning, are already among the most advanced in the world, enabling unprecedented levels of social control.

The United States, meanwhile, remains a strong contender, thanks to its vibrant tech ecosystem and academic institutions. Companies like Google, Microsoft, and OpenAI are at the forefront of AI research, driving innovations in natural language processing, computer vision, and autonomous systems. However, concerns about fragmented regulation and inconsistent government support have raised questions about whether the U.S. can maintain its leadership position.

Other players, such as the European Union, India, and Israel, are also making significant investments in AI, each pursuing strategies aligned with their unique priorities and resources. But while competition can spur innovation, the lack of global coordination poses serious risks, particularly when it comes to safety and ethics.

The Dark Side of Competition: Safety and Ethics on the Sidelines

The AI arms race is characterized by a relentless focus on speed and innovation. In the rush to outpace competitors, organizations often prioritize short-term gains over long-term considerations. This approach creates systems that are not only flawed but also potentially dangerous.

One of the most troubling consequences of this dynamic is the deployment of AI systems without adequate testing or oversight. In 2022, a self-driving car developed by a major automaker was involved in a fatal accident, raising questions about whether the technology had been rushed to market. While the company emphasized its commitment to safety, critics argued that competitive pressure to be the first to achieve full autonomy had overshadowed rigorous testing protocols.

The military sector offers another stark example. Autonomous weapons, often dubbed "killer robots," are being developed by multiple nations, despite widespread concerns about their ethical implications. These systems, powered by AI, can identify and engage targets without human intervention. While proponents argue that they could reduce casualties by minimizing human error, critics warn that they could lower the threshold for conflict, making wars easier to start and harder to control. The lack of international agreements governing the use of such weapons underscores the dangers of unchecked competition.

Even in less overtly dangerous contexts, the prioritization of speed over ethics can have harmful consequences. In 2020, an AI-powered hiring tool used by a multinational corporation was found to discriminate against women and minorities. The system, designed to streamline recruitment, had been trained on biased historical data. Rather than addressing the bias, the company had deployed the tool to gain a competitive edge in hiring efficiency, inadvertently perpetuating inequality.

The Role of Big Tech: Innovators or Gatekeepers?

Big tech companies are both the primary drivers and gatekeepers of the AI arms race. With their vast resources, cutting-edge research labs, and access to global markets, firms like Google, Amazon, and Tencent wield immense influence over the trajectory of AI development. But this concentration of power raises critical questions: Who sets the rules? And who holds these companies accountable?

On one hand, big tech has been responsible for groundbreaking innovations. OpenAI's GPT series, for instance, has revolutionized natural language processing, enabling applications ranging from chatbots to content generation. On the other hand, these same companies have faced criticism for their lack of transparency and their tendency to prioritize profit over societal well-being.

The market dominance of big tech also creates barriers for smaller players. Startups and academic researchers often struggle to compete with the scale and resources of tech giants, limiting the diversity of perspectives in AI development. This consolidation of power risks turning AI into a tool that serves the interests of a few, rather than the needs of the many.

The Challenge of Regulation: Balancing Innovation and Oversight

Regulating AI is a daunting task. Policymakers must strike a delicate balance: fostering innovation while ensuring that the technology is safe, ethical, and fair. Too much regulation risks stifling progress, while too little allows harmful practices to proliferate.

The European Union has taken a proactive approach with its proposed AI Act, which aims to establish comprehensive rules governing the use of AI across various sectors. The act categorizes AI applications by risk level, imposing stricter requirements on high-risk systems, such as those used in healthcare and law enforcement. While the initiative has been praised for its ambition, critics argue that its broad scope could hinder innovation and disproportionately impact smaller companies.

In the United States, regulation has been more fragmented. Federal agencies have issued guidelines for specific industries, such as autonomous vehicles and healthcare, but there is no overarching framework for AI governance. This patchwork approach has led to inconsistencies and loopholes, making it harder to hold organizations accountable for harmful practices.

China, in contrast, has embraced a top-down approach to regulation, leveraging its centralized governance model to implement sweeping policies. In 2021, the government introduced rules aimed at curbing algorithmic abuses, such as excessive data collection and discriminatory practices. However, critics argue that these measures are less about protecting citizens and more about consolidating state control over technology.

The lack of global coordination in AI regulation poses a significant challenge. Without international agreements, nations may engage in regulatory arbitrage, weakening standards in the pursuit of competitive advantage. This dynamic is particularly concerning in areas like autonomous weapons, where the risks of unregulated development extend beyond national borders.

Hope for a Responsible Path Forward

Despite the challenges, there is hope for a more responsible path forward in the AI arms race. Achieving this vision will require collaboration among governments, corporations, and civil society, as well as a commitment to ethical principles that prioritize humanity over ambition.

One promising approach is the development of international norms and agreements. Just as treaties like the Nuclear Non-Proliferation Treaty have helped mitigate the risks of nuclear weapons, similar agreements could govern the development and use of AI. Initiatives like the Global Partnership on AI, which brings together governments, academics, and industry leaders to promote ethical AI, represent a step in the right direction.

Corporate responsibility also plays a critical role. Companies that prioritize ethical AI development can set a standard for the industry, demonstrating that innovation and integrity are not mutually exclusive. For example, Microsoft has established an AI ethics committee to oversee its projects, while Google has committed to not developing AI for autonomous weapons. These efforts, while imperfect, show that it is possible to align business objectives with societal values.

Public advocacy is another powerful tool. By supporting companies and organizations that champion ethical AI, individuals can influence the direction of the field. Consumer demand for transparency, fairness, and safety can push corporations to prioritize these principles, creating a market incentive for responsible innovation.

Finally, education and awareness are essential. As AI becomes increasingly integrated into daily life, it is critical for citizens to understand its capabilities, limitations, and risks. By fostering digital literacy and critical thinking, we can empower individuals to navigate the challenges of the AI age and hold developers and policymakers accountable.

The Long-Term Vision: Collaboration Over Competition

The AI arms race need not be defined by conflict. A more collaborative approach, grounded in shared goals and mutual respect, is both possible and necessary. By focusing on areas of common interest—such as combating climate change, advancing healthcare, and improving education—nations and organizations can harness the power of AI for the greater good.

For example, AI-powered climate models are helping scientists predict and mitigate the impacts of global warming, while machine learning algorithms are accelerating the search for new drugs and treatments. These applications demonstrate the potential of AI to address some of humanity's most pressing challenges. But realizing this potential requires a shift in mindset, from competition to cooperation.

The stakes could not be higher. The choices we make today will shape the future of AI and, by extension, the future of humanity. By prioritizing ethics, transparency, and collaboration, we can ensure that AI serves as a force for progress rather than a source of division. The AI arms race is not just a battle for technological supremacy—it is a test of our collective wisdom and our commitment to building a better world.

Chapter 9
Adaptation and Partnership with AI

Introduction: Humanity's Long History with Technology

In 1440, Johannes Gutenberg's printing press revolutionized the spread of knowledge, empowering individuals to access and disseminate information on a scale previously unimaginable. Yet, the invention was met with skepticism. Critics feared it would undermine traditional scribes, diminish the value of oral storytelling, and flood society with unvetted ideas. Over time, however, the printing press became a cornerstone of progress, enabling the Renaissance, the Enlightenment, and the modern scientific era.

This historical moment serves as a reminder that humanity has always faced uncertainty when confronting transformative technologies. From the industrial revolution to the rise of the internet, each wave of innovation has disrupted existing systems, displaced jobs, and raised existential questions about the future. And yet, humanity has adapted, finding ways to integrate these technologies into daily life while preserving the core values of creativity, empathy, and critical thinking.

Today, artificial intelligence represents the next great technological shift. Unlike previous innovations, however, AI's scale and complexity are unprecedented. It's not just automating tasks; it's reshaping decision-making, creativity, and even human relationships. The stakes are higher than ever, but so is the potential for progress. By adapting thoughtfully and embracing AI as a partner, humanity can harness its power to address pressing challenges, unlock new opportunities, and thrive in an era of unparalleled technological change.

The Nature of Partnership: AI as a Tool, Not a Replacement

At its core, AI is a tool—a set of algorithms designed to process data, identify patterns, and make predictions. But the way we interact with this tool will determine whether it becomes a force for empowerment or disempowerment. The key lies in fostering a mindset of **partnership** rather than replacement.

Take the example of healthcare. AI-powered diagnostic systems, like those developed by Google's DeepMind and IBM Watson, have demonstrated remarkable accuracy in identifying diseases such as cancer and diabetic retinopathy. These systems are not meant to replace doctors but to augment their capabilities, providing insights that help clinicians offer faster and more accurate diagnoses. In this way, AI becomes a partner in care, enhancing human expertise rather than supplanting it.

The same principle applies to creative fields. Generative AI tools like OpenAI's DALL-E and ChatGPT are enabling artists, writers, and designers to explore new ideas, iterate faster, and experiment with styles that were previously out of reach. These tools are not replacing creativity but amplifying it, allowing humans to focus on higher-order tasks such as conceptualization and storytelling.

However, the perception of AI as a partner is not universal. In some industries, workers view AI as a threat, fearing that automation will render their skills obsolete. This fear is not unfounded—AI is already replacing jobs in manufacturing, logistics, and customer service. But history suggests that technological advancements, while disruptive, also create new opportunities. The industrial revolution, for instance, displaced agricultural jobs but gave rise to entirely new industries, from manufacturing to finance.

The challenge today is to ensure that AI-driven disruption leads to a similar rebirth of opportunity. This requires proactive efforts to reskill workers, redesign jobs, and create pathways for individuals to thrive in a world where AI is ubiquitous.

Rethinking Education for an AI-Powered World

Adapting to AI will require a fundamental rethinking of education. Traditional models, which emphasize rote memorization and standardized testing, are ill-suited for a world where AI can perform routine tasks faster and more accurately than humans. Instead, education must focus on fostering the uniquely human skills that AI cannot replicate: creativity, critical thinking, emotional intelligence, and ethical reasoning.

One promising approach is the integration of AI into the classroom as a teaching assistant. Tools like Khan Academy's AI tutor, powered by GPT-4, are already helping students learn at their own pace, offering personalized feedback and adapting to individual learning styles. These tools free teachers from administrative burdens, allowing them to focus on mentoring, inspiring, and addressing the emotional and social needs of their students.

However, the use of AI in education also raises ethical questions. How do we ensure that AI-driven learning systems are free from bias? How do we protect student privacy in an era of data-driven education? And how do we prevent over-reliance on AI, ensuring that students develop critical thinking skills rather than merely accepting algorithmic answers? Addressing these challenges will require collaboration between educators, policymakers, and technologists, as well as ongoing scrutiny of how AI is deployed in schools.

Beyond K-12 education, the rise of AI demands a culture of **lifelong learning**. As industries evolve, workers will need to continually update their skills to remain competitive. Governments and corporations have a critical role to play here, investing in reskilling programs that prepare workers for the jobs of the future. Initiatives like IBM's SkillsBuild and Google's Career Certificates are examples of how public-private partnerships can support this transition, offering accessible and affordable training in areas like data analysis, machine learning, and cloud computing.

The Future of Work: Collaboration Between Humans and Machines

The workplace is one of the most visible arenas where the adaptation to AI is playing out. From chatbots handling customer inquiries to algorithms optimizing supply chains, AI is reshaping how businesses operate. But while automation often dominates the narrative, the more profound transformation lies in how humans and machines are collaborating.

Consider the field of architecture. AI-powered design tools are enabling architects to generate complex structures, optimize energy efficiency, and simulate environmental impacts—all within minutes. But these tools do not diminish the role of the architect; they enhance it. By automating technical calculations, AI allows architects to focus on the creative and human-centric aspects of their work, such as designing spaces that inspire and connect people.

This dynamic is also evident in finance, where AI systems are analyzing market trends, detecting fraud, and even advising clients. While some fear that these systems will replace financial analysts, the reality is more nuanced. AI excels at processing vast amounts of data, but it lacks the intuition, judgment, and relationship-building skills that human analysts bring to the table. The most successful firms are those that leverage AI as a complement to human expertise, creating teams where machines handle the data crunching and humans provide the strategic vision.

However, this vision of collaboration is not guaranteed. Without deliberate effort, AI could exacerbate inequality, creating a divide between those who work alongside technology and those who are displaced by it. Bridging this gap will require not only reskilling initiatives but also a rethinking of workplace culture. Organizations must foster environments where workers feel empowered to learn, adapt, and innovate alongside AI, rather than fearing for their jobs.

Public Policy and the Role of Government

Adapting to AI is not just a technological challenge—it is a societal one. As such, governments have a critical role to play in shaping the policies, regulations, and infrastructure that enable successful adaptation.

One of the most urgent priorities is addressing the economic disruption caused by AI. Automation is expected to displace millions of jobs in the coming decades, particularly in industries like transportation, retail, and manufacturing. While new jobs will emerge, the transition will not be seamless. Governments must invest in social safety nets, such as unemployment benefits and universal basic income, to support workers during periods of displacement.

Regulation is another key area. From ensuring the ethical use of AI in law enforcement to protecting consumer privacy, policymakers must create frameworks that balance innovation with accountability. The European Union's proposed AI Act, which aims to establish clear rules for high-risk AI applications, is an example of how regulation can promote trust while fostering innovation.

At the same time, governments must recognize the global nature of AI. Issues like data privacy, algorithmic bias, and the ethical use of AI transcend national borders, requiring international collaboration. Initiatives like the Global Partnership on AI, which brings together nations to promote responsible AI development, offer a model for how countries can work together to address these challenges.

The Role of Creativity, Empathy, and Human Values

As AI takes on more tasks, there is growing concern that humanity will lose touch with the qualities that make us uniquely human. Creativity, empathy, and ethical reasoning—traits that cannot be coded into algorithms—must remain central to how we navigate the AI era.

This is particularly important in fields like healthcare, where the human touch is irreplaceable. AI can analyze medical images with remarkable accuracy, but it cannot hold a patient's hand, understand their fears, or offer comfort during difficult times. Similarly, in education, AI tutors can provide personalized instruction, but they cannot inspire students or nurture their emotional growth. Preserving these human values requires a deliberate effort to integrate empathy and ethics into how we design and deploy AI systems.

Creativity, too, will play a vital role in shaping the future. While AI can generate art, music, and literature, it lacks the originality and emotional depth of human creators. By embracing AI as a tool for experimentation and exploration, artists and writers can push the boundaries of their craft, creating works that blend human ingenuity with machine precision.

Addressing Global Challenges Through AI Partnership

The ultimate promise of AI lies in its potential to address some of humanity's most pressing challenges. From combating climate change to advancing medical research, AI has the power to transform how we solve global problems. But realizing this potential requires a mindset of partnership—both between humans and AI and among nations, organizations, and individuals.

For example, AI-powered climate models are helping scientists predict the impacts of global warming with unprecedented accuracy, enabling more effective mitigation strategies. In agriculture, AI-driven systems are optimizing irrigation, reducing waste, and improving crop yields, addressing food insecurity in developing countries. These applications demonstrate the transformative potential of AI when used responsibly and collaboratively.

However, the global benefits of AI are not evenly distributed. Wealthy nations and corporations are reaping the lion's share of AI's rewards, while poorer regions risk being left behind. Ensuring equitable access to AI's benefits will require international cooperation, investment in infrastructure, and a commitment to inclusion.

Conclusion: Thriving in an AI-Enhanced World

Adapting to AI is not just about surviving disruption—it's about thriving in a world where human potential is amplified by technology. By rethinking education, fostering collaboration, and prioritizing human values, we can create a future where AI serves as a partner rather than a threat.

The challenges posed by AI are real, but they are not insurmountable. Just as humanity adapted to the printing press, the steam engine, and the internet, we will learn to navigate the complexities of AI. The key is to approach this transition with intentionality, ensuring that progress is guided by empathy, ethics, and a commitment to the greater good.

The age of AI is not the end of human ingenuity—it is the beginning of a new chapter. By embracing partnership and adaptation, we can write a future that is not only technologically advanced but also profoundly human.

Part III – Impact of AI on the Global Job Market (Country-Specific Analysis)

Introduction: A Changing Global Landscape

In 2021, a report by the World Economic Forum estimated that artificial intelligence and automation could displace 85 million jobs globally by 2025. At the same time, the report projected that 97 million new roles could emerge, focused on AI development, data analysis, and new forms of human-machine collaboration. This dual reality—one of displacement and creation—represents the paradox of AI's impact on the global job market.

The effects of AI, however, are not uniform. They vary widely based on a country's economic structure, level of technological development, labor policies, and cultural attitudes toward automation. In the United States, AI is reshaping industries like finance and healthcare, while in China, it's revolutionizing manufacturing and logistics. In developing economies, the focus is on how to leapfrog traditional models of growth using AI, while minimizing the risks of job displacement.

This chapter provides a country-specific analysis of how AI is transforming the global labor market. By examining the unique challenges and opportunities in key regions, we gain a clearer understanding of the broader trends shaping the future of work.

The United States: Innovation and Inequality

The United States has long been a leader in AI research and development, with companies like Google, Microsoft, and OpenAI at the forefront of innovation. This technological dominance has created significant opportunities in high-skill sectors. For example, demand for AI specialists, data scientists, and machine learning engineers has skyrocketed, with salaries for these roles often exceeding six figures.

However, the benefits of AI are not evenly distributed. While the tech sector is thriving, automation is displacing jobs in industries like retail, manufacturing, and transportation. The rise of autonomous vehicles, for instance, threatens the livelihoods of millions of truck drivers, delivery workers, and taxi operators. Similarly, AI-powered chatbots and customer service platforms are reducing demand for call center employees.

The U.S. labor market is also experiencing a growing "skills gap." Many workers lack the training needed to transition into AI-related roles, exacerbating economic inequality. According to a 2022 study by the Brookings Institution, rural and low-income communities are particularly vulnerable to job displacement, as they often lack access to reskilling programs and high-speed internet.

Policy Response:

To address these challenges, the U.S. government and private sector have launched several initiatives. Programs like Google's Career Certificates and IBM's SkillsBuild offer accessible training in fields such as data analysis and cybersecurity. Meanwhile, policymakers are exploring proposals for universal basic income (UBI) and wage subsidies to support workers during periods of transition.

The U.S. experience highlights both the promise and the perils of AI. While the technology is driving innovation and economic growth, it is also deepening existing inequalities. The challenge for policymakers is to ensure that the benefits of AI are shared more broadly across the population.

China: The Automation Powerhouse

China is arguably the world's most aggressive adopter of AI, driven by its government's ambition to dominate the technology by 2030. The country's focus on AI is reshaping its labor market, particularly in manufacturing and logistics, where automation is replacing human workers at an unprecedented scale.

For example, companies like JD.com and Alibaba have introduced fully automated warehouses, where robots manage inventory, pack orders, and even deliver goods. Similarly, autonomous vehicles are being deployed in logistics hubs, reducing reliance on human drivers. While these innovations have boosted efficiency, they have also displaced low-skill workers, who form the backbone of China's labor force.

At the same time, AI is creating new opportunities in high-tech sectors. Cities like Shenzhen and Beijing have become hubs for AI startups, attracting engineers, researchers, and entrepreneurs. The demand for AI talent is so high that some companies are offering salaries that rival those in Silicon Valley.

Policy Response:

The Chinese government is taking a proactive approach to managing the transition. Through initiatives like the Made in China 2025 plan, it is investing heavily in reskilling programs and vocational training. The government is also promoting AI education at all levels, from primary schools to universities, to ensure a steady pipeline of talent.

However, there are concerns about the social impact of widespread automation. In a country where economic stability is closely tied to employment, the displacement of millions of workers could lead to social unrest. Balancing the benefits of AI-driven growth with the need for social cohesion will be one of China's greatest challenges in the coming decades.

European Union: Balancing Innovation and Regulation

The European Union (EU) has taken a cautious but proactive approach to AI, emphasizing ethical considerations and worker protections. While the EU is not as dominant as the U.S. or China in AI innovation, it has made significant strides in sectors like automotive manufacturing, healthcare, and energy.

Germany, for instance, is leveraging AI to modernize its industrial base. Companies like Siemens and Bosch are using machine learning to optimize production processes, reduce waste, and improve safety. Similarly, France is investing in AI for healthcare, with startups developing systems for early disease detection and personalized treatment.

However, automation is also creating challenges, particularly in countries with aging populations and high labor costs. AI-driven efficiency gains are reducing demand for low-skill workers in industries like agriculture and retail, while increasing competition for high-skill roles.

Policy Response:

The EU's approach to AI is guided by its commitment to worker rights and social equity. The proposed AI Act, for example, aims to establish strict rules for high-risk AI applications, ensuring that they meet standards for transparency, accountability, and fairness. At the same time, the EU is investing in reskilling programs, such as the Digital Europe Programme, which aims to train a new generation of AI specialists.

While the EU's emphasis on regulation may slow the pace of AI adoption, it also provides a model for how to balance innovation with social responsibility. By prioritizing ethical considerations, the EU is positioning itself as a leader in responsible AI development.

India: Leapfrogging into the Future

India, with its large and youthful population, stands at a unique crossroads in the AI revolution. While the country is not yet a global leader in AI innovation, it has the potential to leapfrog traditional development models by leveraging AI to address systemic challenges in areas like agriculture, healthcare, and education.

One of the most promising applications of AI in India is in agriculture. Startups like CropIn and Ninjacart are using machine learning to optimize crop yields, reduce waste, and connect farmers directly with markets. Similarly, AI-powered telemedicine platforms are expanding access to healthcare in rural areas, where doctor shortages are severe.

However, India also faces significant risks. Automation is threatening jobs in sectors like business process outsourcing (BPO), which has historically been a major employer. As AI systems become more adept at handling tasks like customer service and data entry, millions of workers could find themselves displaced.

Policy Response:

The Indian government has launched several initiatives to prepare for the AI era. The National AI Strategy, for example, emphasizes the need for skill development, research, and ethical AI deployment. Programs like the Pradhan Mantri Kaushal Vikas Yojana (PMKVY) are providing vocational training to help workers transition into new roles.

India's ability to harness AI will depend on its infrastructure and education systems. Investments in digital connectivity, particularly in rural areas, will be crucial for ensuring that AI's benefits reach all segments of society. By focusing on inclusion and accessibility, India has the potential to turn AI into a tool for empowerment rather than displacement.

Africa: Challenges and Opportunities in a Developing Continent

Africa's relationship with AI is shaped by its status as a developing continent with diverse economies. While some nations, like South Africa and Kenya, are emerging as AI hubs, much of the continent remains focused on addressing basic infrastructure challenges.

AI has the potential to transform key sectors in Africa, particularly agriculture and healthcare. For example, precision farming technologies are helping farmers optimize resource use, while AI-powered diagnostic tools are improving access to healthcare in remote areas. These innovations could play a critical role in addressing food insecurity and public health crises.

However, Africa also faces significant barriers to AI adoption. Many countries lack the infrastructure, funding, and skilled workforce needed to implement AI solutions at scale. Moreover, the risk of job displacement is particularly high in sectors like agriculture and mining, which employ large portions of the population.

Policy Response:

To address these challenges, African governments and international organizations are investing in AI education and infrastructure. Initiatives like the African Union's Digital Transformation Strategy aim to promote digital literacy and create an enabling environment for AI innovation. Partnerships with tech giants, such as Google's AI research lab in Ghana, are also helping to build local expertise.

Africa's experience highlights the importance of global cooperation in the AI era. By fostering partnerships and sharing resources, the international community can help ensure that AI contributes to sustainable development across the continent.

Latin America: Struggling to Keep Pace

Latin America's adoption of AI has been slower compared to other regions, reflecting its economic and political challenges. However, there are bright spots, particularly in countries like Brazil, Mexico, and Chile, where AI is being used to improve public services and drive economic growth.

In Brazil, for example, AI systems are being deployed to monitor deforestation in the Amazon, providing real-time data to conservationists and policymakers. Similarly, Mexico is using AI to combat crime, with predictive policing systems helping law enforcement allocate resources more effectively.

Despite these successes, Latin America faces significant hurdles. High levels of inequality, weak infrastructure, and limited access to education are slowing the region's ability to capitalize on AI. Moreover, the risk of job displacement is particularly acute in industries like manufacturing and agriculture, which employ large segments of the population.

Policy Response:

To address these challenges, Latin American governments are focusing on education and entrepreneurship. Programs like Brazil's AI Strategy and Chile's Start-Up Chile initiative aim to foster innovation and develop local talent. However, much more needs to be done to create an ecosystem that supports AI adoption and mitigates its risks.

Conclusion: Navigating a Global Transition

The impact of AI on the global job market is as diverse as the countries it touches. In some regions, AI is driving innovation and creating high-skill jobs, while in others, it is displacing workers and exacerbating inequality. These dynamics underscore the need for tailored solutions that reflect each country's unique economic, social, and cultural context.

What unites these efforts is the recognition that AI is not just a technological challenge—it is a societal one. By investing in education, fostering collaboration, and prioritizing inclusion, nations can navigate this transition in a way that benefits everyone. The future of work is not predetermined; it is a choice. And with thoughtful adaptation, the AI era can be one of empowerment and progress.

Chapter 10
United States: AI as a Job Disruptor and Creator

Introduction: Leading the AI Revolution

The United States stands at the forefront of the artificial intelligence revolution. Home to global tech leaders like Google, Microsoft, OpenAI, and Amazon, the U.S. has become the epicenter of AI innovation. From generative AI models like ChatGPT to autonomous vehicles and predictive analytics, American companies are defining the cutting edge of technology.

But with great progress comes great complexity. While AI has the potential to drive economic growth, improve efficiency, and create high-paying jobs, it is also a disruptor. The deployment of AI systems is reshaping industries, automating tasks once performed by humans, and deepening economic divides. Jobs in manufacturing, transportation, retail, and administrative roles are particularly vulnerable, while new opportunities are emerging for AI developers, data scientists, and cybersecurity experts.

The U.S. job market is experiencing profound change, with AI serving as both a catalyst for innovation and a source of anxiety. The challenge for policymakers, businesses, and workers is to navigate this transition in a way that maximizes benefits while minimizing harm. This chapter explores the dual nature of AI as both a disruptor and creator of jobs, highlighting key trends, challenges, and strategies for adaptation.

The Disruptive Power of AI

Artificial intelligence is reshaping the American economy by automating repetitive tasks, optimizing workflows, and enabling smarter decision-making. While these advancements boost productivity, they also disrupt traditional employment models, particularly in sectors that rely on routine, manual, or predictable tasks.

1. Manufacturing: The Rise of Smart Factories

Manufacturing has long been a cornerstone of the U.S. economy, employing millions of workers in industries ranging from automotive to electronics. However, the rise of AI-powered robotics and smart factories is transforming the sector. Companies like Tesla and General Motors are using machine learning algorithms to optimize supply chains, predict equipment failures, and automate assembly lines.

For example, Tesla's Gigafactories leverage AI-driven robots to perform tasks such as welding, painting, and quality control. While these systems improve efficiency and reduce costs, they also displace human workers. According to a 2023 report by the Brookings Institution, automation has contributed to the decline of manufacturing jobs in the U.S., particularly in regions like the Midwest, where such roles have historically been concentrated.

2. Transportation: The Road to Autonomy

The transportation industry is another area where AI is making waves. Autonomous vehicles, powered by machine learning and computer vision, promise to revolutionize logistics, delivery, and personal transportation. Companies like Waymo, Uber, and Tesla are testing self-driving cars and trucks, with the potential to replace millions of drivers.

The American Trucking Association estimates that approximately 3.5 million truck drivers could see their roles disrupted by autonomous vehicles in the coming decades. While these technologies have the potential to reduce accidents and lower transportation costs, they also pose significant challenges for a workforce that includes drivers, dispatchers, and warehouse operators.

3. Retail and Administrative Roles: Automating the Everyday

Retail and administrative jobs, which employ tens of millions of Americans, are particularly vulnerable to automation. AI-powered systems are already handling tasks like inventory management, cashiering, and customer service. For instance, Amazon's cashier-less stores use computer vision and sensors to enable customers to shop without interacting with a human employee.

Similarly, administrative roles are being disrupted by AI tools that can schedule meetings, process invoices, and manage customer inquiries. Virtual assistants like Microsoft's Cortana and AI-driven chatbots are replacing traditional office tasks, threatening administrative roles that have long been a reliable source of employment for middle- and lower-income workers.

The Creative Potential of AI

While AI is displacing jobs in some sectors, it is also creating new opportunities in others. The technology is driving demand for highly skilled workers in fields like software development, data science, and cybersecurity. Additionally, AI is enabling innovation in industries such as healthcare, finance, and entertainment, creating roles that didn't exist a decade ago.

1. High-Tech Roles: Building the AI Ecosystem

The rapid growth of AI has led to a surge in demand for technical expertise. AI developers, machine learning engineers, and data scientists are among the most sought-after professionals in the U.S. job market. According to LinkedIn's 2024 Emerging Jobs Report, roles related to AI and data science have grown by over 70% in the past five years.

Companies like OpenAI and Google are offering lucrative salaries to attract top talent, with senior AI researchers earning upwards of $300,000 annually. These roles require advanced skills in programming, mathematics, and algorithm design, making them accessible primarily to workers with specialized education and training.

2. Cybersecurity: Protecting a Digital World

As AI systems become more prevalent, the need for cybersecurity experts has grown exponentially. AI is both a tool for enhancing security and a target for malicious actors, creating a demand for professionals who can protect sensitive data and infrastructure. Cybersecurity roles, such as ethical hackers and penetration testers, are among the fastest-growing jobs in the U.S., with salaries often exceeding six figures.

3. Healthcare: Augmenting Care with AI

AI is transforming the healthcare industry, creating opportunities for professionals who can integrate technology into clinical practice. From AI-powered diagnostic tools to personalized treatment plans, the technology is enabling doctors and nurses to deliver better care. For example, radiologists are using AI algorithms to detect early signs of cancer, while pharmacists are leveraging AI to predict drug interactions.

These advancements are creating new roles for healthcare professionals who can work alongside AI systems, blending technical skills with human empathy and judgment.

Challenges: Inequality and the Skills Gap

While AI is creating new opportunities, it is also exacerbating existing inequalities. The benefits of AI are concentrated among high-skill, high-income workers, while low-skill, low-income workers bear the brunt of job displacement. This dynamic is contributing to a growing divide between those who can adapt to the AI economy and those who are left behind.

1. Income Inequality

The rise of AI is amplifying income inequality in the U.S. Workers in high-tech roles are seeing their salaries soar, while those in low-skill jobs are experiencing wage stagnation or displacement. According to a 2022 report by the Economic Policy Institute, the gap between high- and low-income workers is at its widest point in decades, driven in part by technological advancements.

2. The Skills Gap

One of the biggest barriers to adaptation is the skills gap. Many workers lack the education and training needed to transition into AI-driven roles. For example, while demand for data scientists is growing, only a small percentage of the workforce has the technical expertise required for these positions.

This skills gap is particularly pronounced in rural and low-income communities, where access to education and training programs is limited. Without targeted interventions, these workers risk being permanently left out of the AI economy.

Strategies for Adapting to the AI Era

Adapting to the changes brought by AI will require a coordinated effort across government, industry, and education. By investing in reskilling programs, promoting inclusion, and fostering innovation, the U.S. can ensure that the benefits of AI are shared more broadly.

1. Reskilling and Lifelong Learning

Reskilling is critical for helping workers transition into new roles. Programs like Google's Career Certificates and IBM's SkillsBuild are providing accessible training in fields like data analysis, cloud computing, and cybersecurity. Similarly, community colleges and vocational schools are offering courses in AI-related skills, such as programming and machine learning.

The concept of lifelong learning is also gaining traction. As industries continue to evolve, workers will need to update their skills regularly. Employers can play a role by offering on-the-job training and tuition reimbursement programs, ensuring that their workforce remains competitive.

2. Promoting Inclusion

Ensuring that all Americans benefit from AI will require a focus on inclusion. This means addressing disparities in access to education, technology, and opportunities. Initiatives like Microsoft's Airband Program, which aims to expand broadband access in rural areas, are critical for bridging the digital divide and enabling more workers to participate in the AI economy.

3. Ethical and Responsible AI

Finally, fostering trust in AI is essential for its widespread adoption. This requires a commitment to ethical and responsible AI development. Companies must prioritize transparency, accountability, and fairness, ensuring that AI systems are free from bias and designed to benefit society.

Conclusion: A Future of Opportunity and Challenge

The United States is at the forefront of the AI revolution, driving innovation and shaping the future of work. But this leadership comes with challenges. AI is both a disruptor and a creator, displacing jobs in some industries while generating opportunities in others. Navigating this transition will require a concerted effort to address inequality, close the skills gap, and ensure that AI serves as a force for good.

The future of work in the AI era is not predetermined. It is a choice—one that depends on how we adapt, invest, and collaborate. By embracing the potential of AI while addressing its risks, the United States can lead the way in building a future that is both innovative and inclusive.

Chapter 11
China: Workforce Transformation at Scale

Introduction: The Ambition to Lead

On July 20, 2017, China's State Council released its ambitious "Next Generation Artificial Intelligence Development Plan," outlining the nation's goal to become the global leader in AI by 2030. This strategy is not merely a technological aspiration—it is a cornerstone of China's broader economic and geopolitical ambitions. By marrying AI with its industrial base, urban infrastructure, and governance systems, China aims to transform its economy and cement its position as a global superpower.

Central to this plan is the role of the workforce. With the world's largest population and a diverse economy, China faces unique challenges and opportunities in adapting to the AI revolution. On one hand, automation and AI-driven tools are displacing low-skill manufacturing, customer service, and agricultural jobs. On the other, AI is creating high-skill roles in robotics, smart city technologies, and automation system management.

China's approach to workforce transformation is shaped by its authoritarian governance model, which allows for rapid implementation of top-down policies. However, this model also raises significant ethical concerns, particularly around mass surveillance and privacy. As China navigates this transformation, its success—or failure—will have profound implications not only for its citizens but also for the global economy and the future of work.

The Drivers of China's AI Ambitions

China's unprecedented focus on AI is driven by three key factors: economic growth, global competition, and social stability.

1. Economic Growth

For decades, China's economic engine was powered by low-cost manufacturing. However, rising labor costs and demographic shifts, including a shrinking workforce due to the one-child policy, have forced the country to pivot toward higher-value industries. AI is central to this transition, enabling China to modernize its factories, optimize supply chains, and maintain competitiveness in the global market.

2. Global Competition

China views AI as a strategic technology that will define the balance of power in the 21st century. By dominating AI, the country aims to rival the United States in innovation while reducing its dependence on foreign technologies. Companies like Baidu, Tencent, Alibaba, and Huawei are at the forefront of this effort, investing heavily in AI research, cloud computing, and hardware development.

3. Social Stability

Automation and AI are also seen as tools for maintaining social stability. Smart city technologies, powered by AI, are being deployed to manage urban challenges such as traffic congestion, pollution, and crime. At the same time, AI-driven surveillance systems are being used to monitor and control dissent, ensuring that social unrest does not disrupt the country's development.

Job Losses: The Disruption of Traditional Roles

While AI is driving growth and innovation, it is also displacing millions of workers in traditional industries. The sectors most affected include manufacturing, customer service, and agriculture.

1. Manufacturing: Automation in the Factory of the World

China's dominance as the "factory of the world" is under threat from automation. AI-powered robotics are replacing human workers on assembly lines, particularly in industries like electronics, automotive, and textiles. For example, Foxconn, a major supplier for Apple, has replaced over 100,000 workers with industrial robots in recent years.

This shift is particularly acute in China's industrial heartlands, such as Guangdong and Jiangsu provinces, where millions of low-skill workers depend on manufacturing jobs. While automation has improved efficiency and reduced production costs, it has also left many workers struggling to find alternative employment.

2. Customer Service: The Rise of AI-Driven Interfaces

AI-powered chatbots and voice recognition systems are transforming China's customer service landscape. Companies like Alibaba and JD.com are using natural language processing (NLP) to handle customer inquiries, process orders, and resolve complaints. These systems are faster, cheaper, and more efficient than human agents, leading to widespread job displacement in call centers and service departments.

3. Agriculture: Smart Tools in Rural China

In rural China, AI is being used to modernize agriculture, with technologies such as drone-based crop monitoring, automated irrigation, and predictive analytics. While these innovations have improved productivity, they are also reducing the need for human labor. Traditional farming roles, which once employed a significant portion of the population, are rapidly declining.

Job Gains: AI as a Catalyst for New Opportunities

Despite the displacement of traditional roles, AI is creating new opportunities in high-tech sectors. These roles are concentrated in areas like smart city technologies, robotics development, and automation system management.

1. Smart City Technologies

China is a global leader in smart city development, with AI playing a central role in urban planning, traffic management, and public safety. Cities like Hangzhou, home to Alibaba, have implemented AI-powered traffic control systems that use real-time data to optimize traffic flow, reducing congestion by up to 15%.

This sector is creating jobs for software engineers, data scientists, and urban planners who can design and manage these systems. It is also driving demand for specialists in cybersecurity and data privacy, as smart cities generate vast amounts of sensitive information.

2. Robotics Development

China is the world's largest market for industrial robots, and its domestic robotics industry is growing rapidly. Companies like DJI and Siasun Robotics are developing cutting-edge technologies for applications ranging from logistics to healthcare.

The robotics sector is creating high-paying jobs for engineers, technicians, and researchers. It is also fostering innovation in related fields, such as artificial intelligence, hardware design, and materials science.

3. Automation System Management

As factories become more automated, demand is growing for workers who can manage and maintain these systems. Roles such as automation specialists, machine learning engineers, and system integrators are becoming increasingly important. These positions require advanced technical skills, creating opportunities for workers who can adapt to the new demands of the AI economy.

Challenges: Balancing Progress and Trust

China's rapid adoption of AI comes with significant challenges, both domestically and internationally. These include managing workforce displacement, addressing ethical concerns, and building global trust.

1. Workforce Displacement

The speed of China's AI adoption is leaving many workers behind. The country's vocational training programs are not keeping pace with the scale of job displacement, particularly in rural areas and low-skill industries. Without targeted interventions, millions of workers could face prolonged unemployment, leading to social instability.

2. Ethical Concerns

China's use of AI for mass surveillance has raised significant ethical concerns. Technologies such as facial recognition and social credit systems are being deployed to monitor citizens' behavior, sparking debates about privacy and human rights. While these systems are framed as tools for maintaining order, critics argue that they represent a dystopian misuse of technology.

3. Global Trust Issues

China's AI ambitions have also raised concerns on the global stage. Allegations of intellectual property theft, state-sponsored hacking, and the use of AI for geopolitical influence have damaged the country's reputation. For example, Huawei's role in developing 5G infrastructure has faced scrutiny in several countries, with critics citing national security risks.

Building global trust will require greater transparency and adherence to international norms. China's ability to address these concerns will play a critical role in determining its success as a global AI leader.

Strategies for Workforce Transformation

To navigate the challenges of AI-driven workforce transformation, China is pursuing several strategies, including reskilling initiatives, investment in education, and international collaboration.

1. Reskilling Initiatives

The Chinese government is investing heavily in reskilling programs to prepare workers for new roles in the AI economy. For example, the Ministry of Education has partnered with tech companies to offer vocational training in fields like robotics, data analysis, and AI programming. These programs aim to bridge the gap between displaced workers and emerging opportunities.

2. Investment in Education

China is integrating AI education into its school curriculum, ensuring that the next generation is equipped with the skills needed to thrive in a technology-driven world. Universities like Tsinghua and Peking are establishing AI research centers, while international collaborations are bringing global expertise to Chinese institutions.

3. International Collaboration

Despite tensions with the West, China is seeking to collaborate with international partners on AI research and development. Initiatives like the Belt and Road AI Cooperation Plan aim to promote knowledge sharing and joint innovation, particularly with developing countries.

Conclusion: The Future of Work in China

China's government-led AI strategy is reshaping its workforce at an unprecedented scale. While automation and AI-driven tools are displacing low-skill roles, new opportunities are emerging in high-tech sectors, creating a polarized labor market. The country's ability to manage this transition will depend on its commitment to reskilling, education, and ethical governance.

The challenges are immense, but so are the stakes. If successful, China's AI-driven workforce transformation could serve as a model for other nations, demonstrating how technology can drive economic growth and social progress. However, failure to address the ethical and social implications of AI could undermine these gains, both domestically and globally.

China's journey is a reminder that the future of work is not just about technology—it is about the values and choices that shape its implementation. By prioritizing inclusivity, ethics, and collaboration, China can ensure that AI becomes a tool for empowerment rather than division.

Chapter 12
India: Navigating AI in an Emerging Economy

Introduction: AI as a Growth Catalyst

In March 2023, the Indian government launched the "IndiaAI" program, signaling its intent to position the nation as a leader in artificial intelligence. This initiative is part of a broader strategy to harness AI for economic growth, public services, and social impact. As a country where over 65% of the population is under 35, India is uniquely positioned to ride the AI wave, leveraging its youthful workforce, thriving IT sector, and growing startup ecosystem.

But the road ahead is far from straightforward. While AI offers unprecedented opportunities, it also poses significant risks to employment, particularly in sectors like IT services, customer support, and agriculture. Routine tasks that once powered India's economic rise are now at risk of being automated. At the same time, the country is grappling with infrastructure gaps, data quality issues, and a pressing need for large-scale reskilling to equip workers for the AI era.

This chapter examines how India is navigating the complexities of AI adoption, balancing economic growth with social equity, and exploring how the world's largest democracy is shaping its AI future.

The Role of AI in India's Economic Vision

India's approach to AI is firmly rooted in its developmental priorities. Unlike developed nations, where AI is primarily seen as a tool for optimizing efficiency and driving innovation, India views AI as a means to address fundamental challenges, such as poverty, healthcare access, and education. The government's AI strategy emphasizes three key pillars: economic growth, social impact, and global competitiveness.

1. Economic Growth

India's IT sector, a global leader in outsourcing and software development, views AI as both an opportunity and a threat. Companies like Infosys, TCS, and Wipro are investing heavily in AI to remain competitive in a rapidly evolving global market. AI is being used to automate routine coding, optimize workflows, and reduce operational costs, positioning India as a hub for advanced AI services.

2. Social Impact

AI is being deployed to solve uniquely Indian challenges. For instance, the National Health Stack is leveraging AI to improve healthcare outcomes, while programs like PM-Kisan are using AI-powered analytics to support farmers. From combating malnutrition to improving disaster response, AI is playing a pivotal role in enhancing public services.

3. Global Competitiveness

India is keen to establish itself as a global player in AI development. Initiatives like Startup India and Digital India are fostering innovation, while the Ministry of Electronics and Information Technology (MeitY) is working to attract foreign investment in AI research and development.

Job Losses: The Automation Threat

While AI is driving growth and innovation, it is also disrupting traditional employment models, particularly in sectors that have historically been key drivers of India's economy.

1. IT Services: Automating Routine Tasks

India's $194 billion IT industry, which employs over 4.5 million people, faces significant disruption from AI. Routine tasks like data entry, software testing, and basic coding are increasingly being automated. Companies such as Infosys and TCS are deploying AI-powered tools to reduce reliance on human labor, lowering costs but also threatening jobs.

For instance, chatbots and virtual assistants are replacing human agents in IT helpdesks, while machine learning algorithms are automating quality assurance processes. According to a 2022 report by Nasscom, up to 30% of entry-level IT jobs could be automated by 2030, creating uncertainty for workers who lack advanced skills.

2. Customer Support: Chatbots Take Over

India has long been a global hub for customer support, employing millions in call centers and service roles. However, AI-powered chatbots and voice recognition systems are transforming the industry. Companies like Haptik and Freshworks are developing AI solutions that can handle customer queries with minimal human intervention, reducing the demand for human agents.

3. Agriculture: Precision Farming and Automation

Agriculture, which employs nearly 42% of India's workforce, is also being reshaped by AI. Precision farming technologies, such as automated irrigation and AI-driven pest control, are reducing the need for manual labor. While these innovations improve productivity, they also threaten livelihoods in rural areas, where alternative employment opportunities are limited.

Job Gains: Opportunities in the AI Economy

Despite the disruption, AI is creating new opportunities in emerging sectors, particularly in AI-powered public services, startups, and education.

1. AI-Powered Public Services

India's focus on using AI for social impact is creating jobs in fields like healthcare, education, and infrastructure management. For example, AI-powered diagnostic tools are enabling healthcare workers to deliver better care, particularly in rural areas. Similarly, AI-driven platforms like Diksha are transforming education by providing personalized learning experiences for students.

The government's push for smart cities is also driving demand for AI professionals. From traffic management to waste disposal, AI is being used to optimize urban services, creating roles for data scientists, urban planners, and system integrators.

2. Startups: The Engine of Innovation

India's vibrant startup ecosystem is capitalizing on the AI boom. Companies like Unacademy, Lenskart, and Zomato are integrating AI into their platforms, creating opportunities for developers, engineers, and entrepreneurs. The rise of AI-focused startups, supported by government initiatives like Startup India, is generating high-skill jobs and fostering innovation.

3. Education for Upskilling

The growing demand for AI talent is driving investments in education and training. Platforms like Coursera, edX, and UpGrad are offering courses in machine learning, data science, and AI programming. Additionally, the Skill India program is providing vocational training to help workers transition into AI-related roles.

Challenges: Barriers to AI Adoption

While India has made significant strides in AI, several challenges threaten to limit its potential. These include limited AI infrastructure, data quality concerns, and the need for widespread workforce reskilling.

1. Limited AI Infrastructure

India's AI infrastructure remains underdeveloped compared to global leaders like the U.S. and China. High-performance computing facilities and cloud infrastructure are concentrated in urban centers, leaving rural areas underserved. Additionally, the country's broadband penetration, while improving, is still insufficient to support widespread AI adoption.

2. Data Quality and Privacy Concerns

AI systems rely on large volumes of high-quality data, but India faces challenges in this area. Much of the data generated in India is unstructured, inconsistent, or siloed, making it difficult to use for AI applications. Furthermore, India lacks comprehensive data privacy laws, raising concerns about how personal information is collected and used.

3. Workforce Reskilling

India's workforce is not fully prepared for the demands of the AI economy. While the country produces over 1.5 million engineering graduates annually, only a fraction have the skills needed for AI-related roles. The lack of advanced training programs, particularly in rural areas, exacerbates this gap.

Strategies for Navigating the AI Transition

To fully realize AI's potential, India must address these challenges through targeted strategies, including investments in infrastructure, education, and regulation.

1. Building AI Infrastructure

Expanding AI infrastructure is critical for enabling widespread adoption. The government's National AI Strategy emphasizes investments in high-performance computing facilities, cloud services, and broadband connectivity. Public-private partnerships, such as those involving

Reliance Jio and Google, are playing a key role in bridging infrastructure gaps.

2. Improving Data Ecosystems

Creating robust data ecosystems is essential for AI development. Initiatives like IndiaStack and the National Data and Analytics Platform aim to standardize and democratize access to data, making it easier for researchers and developers to build AI solutions. At the same time, policymakers must prioritize data privacy, enacting laws that protect personal information while enabling innovation.

3. Scaling Reskilling Efforts

Workforce reskilling is perhaps the most urgent priority. Programs like Skill India and PMKVY are providing vocational training in AI-related fields, but these efforts must be scaled to reach millions of workers. Collaborations with tech companies can accelerate this process. For example, Microsoft's partnership with the Ministry of Skill Development and Entrepreneurship aims to train over 1 million people in AI and cloud computing by 2025.

4. Promoting Inclusive Growth

Ensuring that AI benefits all segments of society is critical for maintaining social equity. This includes expanding access to education and technology in rural areas, supporting small businesses, and creating policies that mitigate the impact of job displacement. The government's focus on using AI for social impact, such as through the Aspirational Districts Program, is a step in the right direction.

India's Role in the Global AI Ecosystem

India's AI ambitions extend beyond its borders. As an emerging economic power, the country is positioning itself as a global leader in AI development and application. Initiatives like the India-EU Partnership on Artificial Intelligence and collaborations with organizations like the

United Nations are enhancing India's role in shaping global AI norms and standards.

At the same time, India is exploring how to use AI to address global challenges, such as climate change, public health, and sustainable development. For instance, Indian startups are developing AI-powered solutions for renewable energy management, while researchers are using AI to track and predict the spread of infectious diseases.

Conclusion: A Path Forward

India's journey with AI is a story of both promise and complexity. As the country navigates the challenges of workforce transformation, it must balance economic growth with social equity, innovation with regulation, and ambition with responsibility. The stakes are high, but so are the rewards.

By investing in infrastructure, fostering a culture of lifelong learning, and using AI to address critical social challenges, India can position itself as a global leader in the AI revolution. The country's ability to harness AI's potential while addressing its risks will not only shape its economic future but also serve as a model for other emerging economies.

In the end, India's success in navigating AI will depend not just on technology, but on the values and vision that guide its implementation. By prioritizing inclusion, ethics, and collaboration, India can ensure that AI becomes a tool for empowerment, driving progress for all.

Chapter 13
Europe: Ethical AI and Workforce Adaptation

Introduction: Leading with Ethics in the AI Era

Europe has long been a global leader in setting ethical and regulatory standards, from consumer protections to environmental policies. In the age of artificial intelligence, this tradition continues. As AI transforms industries and reshapes the global workforce, Europe is positioning itself as a leader in "ethical AI," with regulations like the General Data Protection Regulation (GDPR) and the forthcoming AI Act laying the foundation for responsible innovation.

However, this cautious approach to AI adoption comes with trade-offs. While Europe's regulatory framework prioritizes transparency, accountability, and fairness, critics argue that strict rules are slowing innovation and putting European companies at a disadvantage compared to their U.S. and Chinese counterparts. At the same time, diverse markets, languages, and labor laws across the European Union (EU) add layers of complexity to workforce adaptation.

Despite these challenges, Europe is not standing still. The continent is leveraging AI to address societal challenges, from climate change to healthcare, while creating opportunities in emerging fields like AI ethics, compliance, and green technologies. This chapter explores Europe's unique approach to AI, examining how it balances ethical considerations with workforce disruption and adaptation.

The Ethical AI Vision: A Global Standard

At the heart of Europe's AI strategy is the belief that technology should serve humanity. This principle is enshrined in the EU's **Ethics Guidelines for Trustworthy AI**, which emphasize transparency, fairness, and human oversight. The forthcoming **AI Act**, expected to be the first comprehensive AI regulation in the world, builds on these principles, categorizing AI applications by risk and imposing stricter requirements on high-risk systems.

1. GDPR: The Foundation of Responsible AI

The GDPR, introduced in 2018, has become a global benchmark for data protection. By emphasizing user consent, data minimization, and accountability, the GDPR has set the stage for ethical AI development. For example, AI systems trained on European data must comply with strict privacy standards, ensuring that personal information is not misused.

2. The AI Act: Regulating Risk

The AI Act takes GDPR principles a step further, focusing specifically on AI systems. It divides applications into four categories:

Unacceptable Risk: AI systems banned outright (e.g., predictive policing).

High Risk: AI in critical sectors like healthcare and law enforcement, subject to strict oversight.

Limited Risk: Applications like chatbots, requiring basic transparency.

Minimal Risk: AI used in non-critical settings, such as video games.

By establishing clear rules, the AI Act aims to build trust in AI systems while fostering innovation. However, critics argue that these regulations may stifle startups and slow the adoption of AI across industries.

Job Losses: Disruption Across Key Sectors

As in other parts of the world, AI is disrupting traditional industries in Europe, particularly in **manufacturing**, **administrative work**, and **transportation**. These sectors, which have historically provided stable employment, are now at the forefront of automation.

1. Manufacturing: Automation in Industry 4.0

Europe's manufacturing sector, known for its precision and quality, is undergoing a transformation driven by **Industry 4.0**—the integration of AI, robotics, and IoT in production processes. Countries like Germany, with its strong industrial base, are leading this shift. For example, Siemens has implemented AI-powered systems in its factories to optimize energy use, reduce waste, and improve efficiency.

While these innovations enhance productivity, they also reduce the need for human labor. Routine tasks such as assembly, quality control, and material handling are increasingly performed by robots, displacing workers in low-skill roles. According to a 2022 report by the European Commission, automation could affect up to 12 million manufacturing jobs across the EU by 2035.

2. Administrative Work: The Rise of AI Assistants

Administrative roles, which employ millions across Europe, are also under threat. AI-powered tools like chatbots, virtual assistants, and automated scheduling systems are replacing routine tasks such as data entry, document processing, and customer service. For instance, the Danish government has introduced AI systems to streamline public administration, reducing the need for human intervention in repetitive processes.

3. Transportation: Autonomous Systems on the Horizon

Europe's transportation sector is being reshaped by autonomous vehicles and AI-powered logistics. Companies like Volvo and Daimler are developing self-driving trucks, while airlines are using AI to optimize flight routes and reduce fuel consumption. These advancements, while beneficial for efficiency, threaten jobs in trucking, shipping, and public transit. The International Transport Forum estimates that automation could displace up to 30% of European transportation jobs by 2040.

Job Gains: Opportunities in Emerging Fields

While AI is displacing jobs in traditional sectors, it is also creating opportunities in new and emerging fields. Europe is investing heavily in areas such as **AI ethics**, **green technologies**, and **personalized medicine**, which align with its values of sustainability and social responsibility.

1. AI Ethics and Compliance

Europe's emphasis on ethical AI is creating demand for professionals who can navigate the regulatory landscape. Roles such as AI compliance officers, data protection specialists, and ethics consultants are emerging as critical components of the AI workforce. These positions require expertise in both technology and law, blending technical skills with a deep understanding of ethical principles.

For example, the Netherlands-based company Aigency provides AI audit services, helping organizations ensure that their systems comply with GDPR and other regulations. Similarly, universities across Europe are introducing degree programs in AI ethics and governance to prepare the next generation of professionals.

2. Green AI Applications

Europe's commitment to sustainability is driving innovation in **green AI**—the use of artificial intelligence to combat climate change and promote environmental stewardship. AI is being used to optimize renewable energy grids, predict weather patterns, and monitor deforestation. For instance:

In Spain, AI-powered systems are helping wind farms optimize energy production.

In Finland, startups are using AI to track carbon emissions and develop carbon-neutral technologies.

These efforts are creating jobs in fields like environmental data analysis, renewable energy management, and sustainable urban planning.

3. Personalized Medicine and Healthcare Innovation

Healthcare is another sector where AI is creating significant opportunities. Personalized medicine, which tailors treatments to individual patients based on genetic and lifestyle factors, is becoming a reality thanks to AI. Companies like Sophia Genetics in Switzerland are using machine learning to analyze genetic data, helping doctors diagnose diseases more accurately and prescribe targeted treatments.

The rise of telemedicine and AI-powered diagnostics is also generating demand for healthcare professionals who can integrate technology into clinical practice. For example, radiologists are using AI to detect early signs of cancer, while general practitioners are leveraging AI to predict patient outcomes.

Challenges: Balancing Ethics, Innovation, and Fragmentation

Europe's approach to AI is shaped by its commitment to ethics and social responsibility, but this comes with challenges that could limit its global competitiveness.

1. Slower Innovation Due to Regulations

While regulations like the GDPR and AI Act promote trust, they also impose compliance costs that can stifle innovation. Startups, in particular, struggle to navigate the complex regulatory landscape, which puts them at a disadvantage compared to competitors in less regulated markets like the U.S. and China. According to a 2023 report by the European

Investment Bank, venture capital funding for AI startups in Europe lags behind other regions, partly due to regulatory hurdles.

2. Market Fragmentation

Europe's diversity, often a strength, poses challenges in the context of AI. Differences in language, labor laws, and market conditions create barriers to scaling AI solutions across the continent. For example, an AI system developed in Germany may need significant modifications to comply with regulations in France or Italy. This fragmentation limits the efficiency of AI deployment and slows adoption.

3. Skills Gap and Workforce Reskilling

While Europe has a strong tradition of education and vocational training, it faces a growing skills gap in AI-related fields. A 2022 report by Eurostat found that only 19% of EU workers have digital skills, far below the levels needed for widespread AI adoption. Reskilling efforts, while underway, must be scaled to meet the demands of the AI economy.

Strategies for Workforce Adaptation

To navigate the challenges of AI-driven disruption, Europe is pursuing several strategies focused on education, investment, and international collaboration.

1. Reskilling and Lifelong Learning

Europe is prioritizing workforce reskilling to help workers transition into emerging roles. Initiatives like the **Digital Skills Agenda for Europe** and the **European Social Fund Plus (ESF+)** aim to provide training in AI, data science, and digital literacy. Countries like Germany and France are also offering tax incentives to companies that invest in employee upskilling.

2. Supporting Startups and Innovation

To foster innovation, the EU is increasing funding for AI research and startups. The **Horizon Europe** program, with a budget of €95.5 billion, includes significant investments in AI-related projects. Additionally, initiatives like the **European Innovation Council (EIC)** are providing grants and equity investments to high-potential startups.

3. Promoting Diversity and Inclusion

Europe is committed to ensuring that AI benefits all segments of society. This includes promoting diversity in AI development and addressing biases in algorithms. Programs like **Women in Digital** aim to increase female participation in tech, while organizations like AlgorithmWatch are advocating for greater transparency in AI systems.

4. Strengthening International Collaboration

Europe recognizes that AI is a global challenge requiring global solutions. The EU is working with international partners, including the United States and Japan, to develop shared standards and frameworks for ethical AI. Initiatives like the **EU-U.S. Trade and Technology Council** are fostering collaboration on issues such as data governance and AI safety.

Conclusion: A Model for Responsible Innovation

Europe's approach to AI is unique in its emphasis on ethics, social responsibility, and sustainability. While this cautious strategy may slow innovation in the short term, it positions Europe as a global leader in responsible AI development. By prioritizing trust, transparency, and inclusivity, Europe is setting a standard that other regions may eventually follow.

The challenges of workforce disruption, regulatory complexity, and market fragmentation are significant, but they are not insurmountable. Through strategic investments in education, innovation, and collaboration, Europe can navigate these challenges and ensure that AI serves as a force for good.

As the world grapples with the implications of AI, Europe's vision offers a powerful reminder: Technology is not an end in itself—it is a means to enhance human well-being. By staying true to this principle, Europe can lead the way in shaping an AI-driven future that benefits everyone.

Chapter 14
Rest of the World: Opportunities and Challenges

Introduction: A World of Contrasts

Artificial intelligence is reshaping the global economy, but its impact varies dramatically across regions. While developed economies like the U.S., Europe, and China leverage AI to drive innovation and industrial efficiency, much of the rest of the world is still grappling with basic infrastructure, uneven technological access, and limited investment in AI. For many developing nations, AI represents both a promise and a threat: a tool for solving entrenched societal problems, but also a driver of economic disparities.

From Africa and South America to the Middle East and Southeast Asia, the adoption of AI reflects a world in transition. In some regions, AI is transforming sectors like agriculture, healthcare, and education, creating opportunities for growth and development. In others, it is displacing workers in traditional industries like low-skill manufacturing and farming, exacerbating unemployment and inequality. The challenges of limited infrastructure, brain drain, and a lack of skilled talent further complicate the picture.

This chapter explores the uneven landscape of AI adoption across the developing world, highlighting its opportunities, challenges, and implications for workforce transformation.

AI Adoption: Uneven and Fragmented

The pace of AI adoption varies widely across regions, reflecting differences in economic development, governmental priorities, and technological infrastructure. While some countries are making impressive strides, others lag behind due to resource constraints and lack of investment.

1. Africa: Leapfrogging with Mobile Technologies

Africa's AI story is one of leapfrogging—skipping traditional stages of technological development to adopt cutting-edge solutions. Mobile technology is at the heart of this transformation. With over 600 million mobile phone users, Africa is leveraging AI to deliver services in sectors like banking, healthcare, and agriculture. For example:

- **Mobile Banking**: Platforms like M-Pesa in Kenya use AI to offer credit scoring, fraud detection, and personalized financial services.
- **Agriculture**: Startups like Aerobotics in South Africa use AI-powered drones to help farmers monitor crop health and optimize yields.

Despite these successes, Africa faces significant barriers to widespread AI adoption, including limited internet access, unreliable electricity, and a shortage of skilled AI professionals.

2. South America: AI for Governance and Resources

South America is using AI to address systemic challenges such as corruption, deforestation, and resource management. In Brazil, AI systems are being deployed to monitor illegal logging in the Amazon, while in Colombia, AI is helping authorities detect tax evasion. However, the region's reliance on low-skill manufacturing and agriculture leaves millions vulnerable to job displacement as automation takes hold.

3. Middle East: Balancing Innovation and Tradition

The Middle East is embracing AI through massive investments in smart city projects and digital transformation. Countries like the United Arab Emirates (UAE) and Saudi Arabia are leading the charge. For example:

The UAE's **AI Strategy 2031** aims to integrate AI into healthcare, education, and government services.

Saudi Arabia's **NEOM project**, a $500 billion smart city initiative, relies heavily on AI for urban planning and infrastructure.

However, the oil-dependent economies of the region face challenges in transitioning their workforces to AI-driven industries, particularly as automation threatens traditional energy and construction jobs.

4. Southeast Asia: Manufacturing Meets AI

Southeast Asia's economies, heavily reliant on manufacturing, are at the forefront of AI-driven industrial automation. Countries like Vietnam, Indonesia, and Thailand are integrating AI into supply chains and logistics. At the same time, startups in these nations are using AI to tackle challenges in healthcare, education, and e-commerce.

Job Losses: Vulnerable Sectors

The vulnerability of developing nations to AI-driven job displacement stems from their reliance on low-skill, labor-intensive industries. Sectors like agriculture, manufacturing, and extractive industries are particularly at risk.

1. Agriculture: Mechanization and AI Integration

Agriculture remains a cornerstone of many developing economies, employing a significant portion of the workforce. However, AI-powered tools such as automated irrigation systems, pest control drones, and yield prediction models are displacing manual labor. For instance:

In Africa, AI-driven platforms like Zenvus analyze soil conditions and suggest planting strategies, reducing the need for human intervention.

In South America, agribusinesses are adopting machine learning to optimize crop rotation and harvest timing.

While these technologies improve efficiency, they also marginalize small-scale farmers who lack the resources to adopt AI.

2. Low-Skill Manufacturing: Automation in Factories

Low-skill manufacturing has traditionally been a key driver of economic growth in regions like Southeast Asia and South America. However, AI-powered robotics are rapidly automating assembly lines, reducing the demand for human labor. For example:

- In Vietnam, textile factories are using AI to automate sewing and cutting processes.
- In Mexico, automotive plants are deploying robots for tasks like welding and painting.

The result is a shrinking pool of jobs for workers with limited education and technical training.

3. Extractive Industries: Mining and Oil

AI is also disrupting extractive industries, particularly in resource-rich regions like Africa and the Middle East. Predictive maintenance systems, automated drilling rigs, and AI-powered safety monitoring are reducing the need for human workers in mines and oil fields.

Job Gains: Emerging Opportunities

While AI is displacing jobs in traditional sectors, it is also creating new opportunities in emerging fields. Developing nations are leveraging AI to address societal challenges and foster innovation in areas like mobile banking, education, healthcare, and smart cities.

1. Mobile Banking and Financial Inclusion

AI is revolutionizing financial services in regions where traditional banking infrastructure is weak. Mobile banking platforms are using AI to provide credit scoring, fraud detection, and personalized savings plans. For example:

- In Kenya, M-Pesa uses AI to expand access to loans and savings accounts.
- In Nigeria, startups like Carbon are leveraging machine learning to assess credit risk and offer microloans.

These innovations are creating jobs for software developers, data scientists, and fintech entrepreneurs.

2. Edtech: Transforming Education

AI-powered edtech platforms are addressing educational challenges in developing nations, such as teacher shortages and low literacy rates. For instance:

- In India, EdTech uses AI to personalize learning experiences for students.
- In Rwanda, the government is partnering with edtech firms to provide AI-driven tools for rural schools.

These initiatives are creating roles for educators, instructional designers, and AI developers.

3. Telemedicine and Healthcare Innovation

AI is playing a critical role in expanding access to healthcare in underserved regions. Telemedicine platforms are using AI to diagnose diseases, recommend treatments, and monitor patient health remotely. For example:

- In Ghana, Zipline uses AI-powered drones to deliver medical supplies to remote areas.

- In Brazil, AI systems are helping doctors predict disease outbreaks and allocate resources more effectively.

These innovations are generating jobs in healthcare technology, logistics, and data analysis.

4. Smart Cities: Building the Future

Smart city projects in the Middle East, Africa, and Southeast Asia are creating demand for professionals who can design, implement, and manage AI-driven infrastructure. For example:

- In Dubai, the Smart Dubai initiative is using AI for traffic management, waste disposal, and public safety.
- In Indonesia, Jakarta's smart city program leverages AI to monitor air quality and reduce congestion.

These projects are generating roles for urban planners, system integrators, and AI specialists.

Challenges: Barriers to AI Adoption

Despite the opportunities AI presents, developing nations face significant challenges in adopting the technology and transforming their workforces.

1. Limited Infrastructure

Many regions lack the technological infrastructure needed for AI adoption. Challenges include unreliable electricity, low internet penetration, and insufficient access to high-performance computing. For example:

- In sub-Saharan Africa, only 28% of the population has access to the internet, limiting the potential for AI-driven solutions.
- In rural South America, poor connectivity hampers the deployment of AI-powered agricultural tools.

2. Brain Drain

The global demand for AI talent is creating a brain drain in developing nations, as skilled professionals migrate to higher-paying jobs in developed countries. This exodus leaves local industries struggling to implement AI solutions.

3. Lack of Skilled Talent

Even within developing nations, there is a shortage of workers with the skills needed for AI development and implementation. Educational systems in many regions have not yet adapted to the demands of the AI economy, leaving workers unprepared for emerging roles.

4. Ethical Concerns and Data Privacy

The use of AI in developing nations raises ethical questions, particularly around data privacy and algorithmic bias. In regions with weak regulatory frameworks, there is a risk that AI systems could reinforce existing inequalities or be misused for surveillance and control.

Strategies for Workforce Transformation

To harness AI's potential while addressing its challenges, developing nations must adopt targeted strategies focused on infrastructure, education, and international collaboration.

1. Investing in Infrastructure

Governments and international organizations must prioritize investments in AI infrastructure, including internet connectivity, electricity, and cloud computing. Public-private partnerships can accelerate progress in this area. For example:

- Google's **Equiano subsea cable** is improving internet access in Africa.

- The World Bank is funding electrification projects in rural areas to support digital inclusion.

2. Scaling Education and Reskilling

Educational systems must be reformed to prepare workers for AI-driven industries. This includes introducing AI and digital literacy into school curriculums and scaling reskilling programs for displaced workers. Initiatives like the African Development Bank's **Coding for Employment** program are a step in the right direction.

3. Fostering Local Innovation

Developing nations should encourage homegrown innovation by supporting startups and small businesses. Incubators, grants, and tax incentives can help entrepreneurs develop AI solutions tailored to local challenges. For example, Rwanda's **Kigali Innovation City** is fostering a vibrant tech ecosystem.

4. Strengthening International Partnerships

Collaboration with international organizations and tech leaders can provide access to funding, expertise, and technology. Initiatives like the United Nations' **AI for Good Global Summit** are fostering dialogue and knowledge sharing between developed and developing nations.

Conclusion: A Path Forward

The adoption of AI in the developing world is a story of contrasts—of opportunities and challenges, progress and barriers. For regions like Africa, South America, and the Middle East, AI offers a chance to leapfrog traditional development models and address pressing societal challenges. But realizing this potential requires overcoming significant obstacles, from limited infrastructure to brain drain.

The future of AI in the developing world will depend on the choices made today. By investing in education, fostering local innovation, and building partnerships, these nations can ensure that AI becomes a tool for empowerment rather than exclusion. As the world navigates the AI revolution, the voices and experiences of the developing world will be critical in shaping a more inclusive and equitable future.

Part IV: The New Labor Market

The global labor market is poised for unprecedented transformation by 2030, as artificial intelligence becomes an integral part of industries worldwide. While the pace of adoption and its effects will vary across regions and sectors, the overarching themes of disruption, creation, and adaptation will define the decade ahead. This section outlines key projections for the labor market by 2030, highlighting emerging trends, opportunities, and challenges.

1. Automation Will Reshape Millions of Jobs

By 2030, automation powered by AI will fundamentally restructure labor markets, particularly in industries reliant on repetitive, rules-based tasks. According to a McKinsey Global Institute report, as many as **400 million jobs globally** could be displaced, with certain industries feeling the impact more acutely:

- **Manufacturing**: Automation of assembly lines, quality control, and logistics will reduce reliance on human labor. Advanced robotics will replace many low-skill positions, while high-skill roles in robotics programming and maintenance will grow.
- **Retail and Customer Service**: AI chatbots, automated checkout systems, and personalized online shopping experiences will eliminate millions of cashier and service roles.
- **Transportation and Logistics**: The rise of autonomous vehicles, drones, and AI-optimized supply chains will disrupt driving and warehousing jobs, with pilot projects in self-driving trucks becoming mainstream by the late 2020s.
- **Clerical and Administrative Work**: Tasks like data entry, invoicing, and scheduling will increasingly be handled by AI-driven tools, reducing the demand for clerical workers.

While automation will improve productivity and reduce costs for businesses, its displacement effects will disproportionately impact workers in low-skill, repetitive jobs, particularly in developing nations and rural areas.

2. The Rise of Hybrid Work Models

The COVID-19 pandemic accelerated the adoption of remote and hybrid work models, a trend that will continue to evolve through 2030. AI-powered tools will enhance collaboration in distributed teams, enabling seamless communication and productivity regardless of location. Key developments include:

- **AI-Driven Workflows**: Virtual assistants, predictive analytics, and automated reporting tools will optimize workflows, allowing employees to focus on creative and strategic tasks.
- **Global Talent Marketplaces**: AI will enable companies to tap into talent pools across borders, particularly for specialized skills like data science and machine learning. This will create opportunities for professionals in developing countries to participate in the global economy.
- **Resilience in Crises**: AI tools will help organizations adapt to disruptions, such as pandemics or geopolitical crises, by enabling remote operations and supply chain resilience.

Hybrid work models will also create opportunities for women, caregivers, and people with disabilities, offering greater flexibility and inclusivity in the workforce.

3. New Job Categories Will Emerge

While automation will displace some jobs, it will also create entirely new categories of employment. By 2030, many roles that do not currently exist will become mainstream, driven by advances in AI, robotics, and data science. Emerging job categories include:

- **AI Specialists**: As AI adoption grows, roles for machine learning engineers, natural language processing experts, and AI ethicists will expand across industries.
- **Green Tech and Sustainability Roles**: AI is driving innovation in renewable energy, energy efficiency, and environmental

monitoring. Roles in carbon capture, smart grid management, and climate modeling will grow significantly.

- **Healthcare AI Professionals**: Personalized medicine, AI-powered diagnostics, and telemedicine will create demand for healthcare workers who can integrate AI into clinical workflows.
- **Cybersecurity Experts**: As AI becomes ubiquitous, protecting AI systems from cyber threats will become a critical priority, creating roles for cybersecurity analysts, ethical hackers, and AI safety specialists.
- **AI Ethics and Compliance Officers**: Regulation of AI systems will generate demand for professionals who can ensure compliance with ethical guidelines and legal standards, particularly in heavily regulated regions like Europe.

According to the World Economic Forum, by 2030, the global economy could see the creation of over **97 million new jobs** in AI-related fields, offsetting some of the displacement caused by automation.

4. Lifelong Learning and Reskilling Will Become Essential

The rapid pace of AI-driven change will make lifelong learning a necessity, not a choice, for workers across all industries. By 2030, traditional education systems will need to be reimagined to prepare individuals for careers in the AI era. Key trends include:

- **AI in Education**: Adaptive learning platforms will use AI to personalize education, tailoring content to individual skills and learning styles. Platforms like Coursera, Khan Academy, and Skillshare are early examples of this trend.
- **Corporate Reskilling Programs**: Companies will increasingly invest in reskilling their workforce to remain competitive. For example, Amazon's Upskilling 2025 initiative and Google's certification programs are likely to be replicated across industries.

- **Government-Led Reskilling Initiatives**: Governments will play a critical role in workforce transformation by funding vocational training and creating incentives for lifelong learning. For instance, Singapore's SkillsFuture program provides citizens with credits to pursue AI and digital skills training.

By 2030, job seekers will be expected to continually update their skills, with a focus on technical competencies (e.g., coding, data analysis) and soft skills (e.g., creativity, adaptability).

5. Regional Disparities Will Deepen

AI adoption will widen the gap between regions that have the infrastructure, talent, and capital to invest in AI and those that do not. By 2030, significant disparities will emerge between developed and developing economies, as well as between urban and rural areas.

Developed Economies

- Countries like the U.S., China, and members of the European Union will lead in AI adoption, benefiting from robust infrastructure, research ecosystems, and access to capital.
- These regions will see significant growth in high-skill jobs, such as AI development, cybersecurity, and green technologies, while experiencing job losses in traditional sectors like manufacturing and transportation.

Developing Economies

- Developing nations, particularly in Africa, South Asia, and Latin America, will face challenges in scaling AI adoption due to limited infrastructure, brain drain, and lack of skilled talent.
- However, mobile technologies, telemedicine, and edtech platforms will provide leapfrogging opportunities, enabling these regions to address critical societal challenges like financial inclusion and access to healthcare.

Urban vs. Rural

- Urban areas, with better access to infrastructure and education, will benefit disproportionately from AI-driven job creation.
- Rural areas, particularly those reliant on agriculture and low-skill manufacturing, will face higher risks of job displacement and slower recovery.

Efforts to bridge these divides—through public-private partnerships, targeted investments, and global collaboration—will be critical to achieving equitable growth by 2030.

6. Ethical AI and Regulation Will Shape the Labor Market

As AI systems become more pervasive, governments, businesses, and international organizations will increasingly focus on regulating their use to ensure fairness, transparency, and accountability. Key developments by 2030 will include:

- **Global AI Standards**: International frameworks for ethical AI, led by organizations like the United Nations and the OECD, will set guidelines for responsible AI deployment. These standards will influence hiring practices, workforce diversity, and algorithmic fairness.
- **AI Audits and Compliance**: Companies will be required to conduct audits of their AI systems to identify and mitigate biases, particularly in hiring algorithms and decision-making tools.
- **Worker Protections**: Governments will introduce policies to protect workers from displacement, including unemployment benefits, wage subsidies, and regulations on the use of AI in hiring and surveillance.

Ethical AI will not only shape the rules of the labor market but also create new opportunities for professionals in AI ethics, compliance, and governance.

7. A More Inclusive and Flexible Workforce

By 2030, the labor market will become more inclusive and flexible, driven by advancements in AI and the ongoing evolution of work. Key trends include:

- **Remote Work at Scale**: AI-powered tools will enable seamless remote work, allowing companies to tap into talent pools from underrepresented regions and communities.
- **Gig Economy Expansion**: The gig economy will grow, with AI platforms connecting workers to short-term, high-skill opportunities. However, this will require stronger protections for gig workers to ensure fair pay and benefits.
- **Inclusivity**: AI will help break down barriers to workforce participation for women, people with disabilities, and underrepresented minorities. For instance, AI accessibility tools like real-time transcription and translation will enable more people to contribute to the global economy.

Conclusion: Building a Resilient Labor Market

The labor market of 2030 will be one of constant change, driven by the dual forces of disruption and innovation. While AI will displace millions of jobs, it will also create new opportunities for those who can adapt. The key to navigating this transition lies in collaboration between governments, businesses, and individuals.

- **Governments** must invest in education, infrastructure, and social safety nets to support workers during the transition.
- **Businesses** must prioritize workforce development, ethical AI practices, and inclusivity in hiring and innovation.
- **Workers** must embrace lifelong learning, reskilling, and adaptability to thrive in the AI-driven economy.

By 2030, the world will have the opportunity to create a labor market that is not only more efficient but also more inclusive, sustainable, and resilient. The choices made today will determine whether AI becomes a tool for empowerment or a source of inequality—a challenge, and a promise, for all of humanity.

Chapter 15
Jobs That Change, Jobs That Grow

The rise of artificial intelligence (AI) is reshaping the global labor market in profound ways, not by simply replacing jobs but by transforming how we work, the skills we need, and the opportunities available. Some traditional roles are disappearing, while others are evolving in response to new technologies. At the same time, entirely new professions are emerging, driven by the demands of an AI-driven economy.

To navigate this transformation, it is critical to understand which types of jobs are most vulnerable to automation, which are adapting to AI, and which are set to grow in the coming decades. This chapter explores the two central dynamics of AI's impact on employment: Jobs That Change and **Jobs That Grow.**

Jobs That Change

The Evolution of Traditional Roles

AI is less about outright job replacement and more about job transformation. Many roles will not disappear but will undergo significant changes as AI tools enhance human productivity and capabilities. These changes are occurring across industries, from administrative work to manufacturing, logistics, and creative fields.

1. Administrative Roles: From Routine to Strategic

Administrative professionals—such as office managers, executive assistants, and clerical staff—are among the first to feel the effects of AI. Tasks such as scheduling, data entry, and reporting, historically time-consuming and repetitive, are increasingly automated by tools like virtual assistants, automated scheduling software, and natural language processing (NLP) systems.

Key Changes:

- **Automation of Routine Tasks:** AI-powered tools like Microsoft's Cortana or Google Assistant can schedule meetings, send reminders, and update calendars without human intervention.
- **Focus on Strategy and Coordination:** Freed from repetitive tasks, administrative professionals can focus on higher-value activities, such as managing team workflows, coordinating cross-departmental projects, and fostering organizational culture.

Example in Practice:

In a mid-sized company, an AI system might handle invoice processing and payroll, allowing HR staff to focus on employee engagement and retention strategies.

2. Manufacturing and Logistics: Humans and Machines Working Together

The manufacturing and logistics industries are undergoing a massive transformation as AI and robotics automate repetitive, physical tasks. From assembly lines to warehouse operations, automation is improving efficiency while reshaping the roles of human workers.

Key Changes:

- **AI-Assisted Decision-Making:** Human workers are increasingly required to oversee and manage AI-powered systems, making decisions based on real-time data insights provided by these tools.
- **Maintenance and Optimization:** Workers are needed to maintain, troubleshoot, and optimize automated systems, requiring a blend of technical and mechanical skills.

- **Collaborative Robotics:** In factories and warehouses, "cobots" (collaborative robots) work alongside humans, assisting with tasks like lifting heavy objects or assembling intricate components.

Example in Practice:

At companies like Amazon, warehouse workers now supervise AI-driven robots that transport packages. These workers ensure the robots function smoothly and adapt to unexpected challenges, such as equipment malfunctions or changes in delivery schedules.

3. Healthcare: Augmenting Human Expertise

AI is revolutionizing healthcare by improving diagnostics, streamlining administrative processes, and enabling personalized treatments. However, these advancements do not replace human healthcare providers—they enhance their ability to deliver care.

Key Changes:

- **Diagnostics and Decision Support:** AI tools can analyze medical images, predict patient outcomes, and recommend treatment plans, allowing doctors to focus on complex cases requiring human judgment.
- **Automating Administrative Work:** AI systems handle tasks like appointment scheduling, patient record management, and billing, freeing up healthcare workers to spend more time with patients.
- **Telemedicine and Remote Monitoring:** AI-powered platforms enable doctors to consult with patients remotely, expanding access to healthcare in underserved areas.

Example in Practice:

AI-based diagnostic tools, such as IBM Watson Health, assist radiologists by identifying early signs of cancer in medical imaging, reducing the time required for diagnosis and improving accuracy.

4. Creative Fields: AI as a Co-Creator

Even in fields traditionally considered immune to automation—such as art, writing, and music—AI is playing an increasingly significant role. Rather than replacing creative professionals, AI acts as a collaborative tool, enabling faster and more innovative work.

Key Changes:

- **Content Generation:** AI tools like OpenAI's ChatGPT or DALL·E generate text, images, and designs, serving as a starting point for human creativity.
- **Enhanced Productivity:** Creative professionals can use AI to automate repetitive tasks, such as editing, formatting, or creating templates, allowing them to focus on the conceptual aspects of their work.
- **New Forms of Creativity:** AI opens up possibilities for entirely new art forms, such as generative art, where algorithms create unique visual designs or soundscapes.

Example in Practice:

In advertising, AI tools generate multiple variations of ad copy or visuals, which human marketers then refine based on brand guidelines and audience preferences.

Jobs That Grow

While many traditional roles are evolving, entirely new jobs are being created to meet the demands of an AI-driven economy. These roles span industries and require skills that did not exist a decade ago. Below, we explore some of the most prominent emerging job categories.

1. AI Trainers: Teaching Machines to Think

AI systems require vast amounts of labeled data to learn and improve. AI trainers play a critical role in this process by curating datasets, labeling images, and teaching AI to interpret human behavior.

Key Responsibilities:

- Annotating data to train AI algorithms (e.g., labeling objects in images or identifying sentiment in text).
- Teaching AI systems to recognize context and nuance in human interactions, such as voice tone or cultural references.
- Continuously updating training data to improve AI accuracy.

Example in Practice:

AI trainers working for self-driving car companies, such as Tesla or Waymo, label millions of images of roads, pedestrians, and vehicles to ensure the AI can navigate safely in real-world conditions.

2. Ethics Officers: Guiding Responsible AI Use

As organizations adopt AI systems, the need for ethical oversight has become increasingly important. Ethics officers ensure that AI aligns with organizational values, complies with regulations, and avoids harm to individuals or society.

Key Responsibilities:

- Assessing the ethical implications of AI applications, such as bias, privacy, and fairness.
- Developing guidelines and policies for responsible AI use.
- Collaborating with legal and technical teams to address potential risks.

Example in Practice:

An ethics officer at a healthcare company might evaluate an AI diagnostic tool to ensure it provides equitable outcomes for patients of different ethnicities and socioeconomic backgrounds.

3. Human-AI Interaction Specialists: Designing Seamless Collaboration

To maximize the benefits of AI, humans and machines must work together effectively. Human-AI interaction specialists design interfaces, workflows, and systems that enable smooth collaboration between people and AI.

Key Responsibilities:

- Developing intuitive user interfaces for AI tools.
- Studying how humans interact with AI and identifying areas for improvement.
- Ensuring that AI systems are accessible and easy to use for non-technical users.

Example in Practice:

At a customer service company, a human-AI interaction specialist might design a chatbot interface that seamlessly transitions complex queries to a human agent, ensuring a positive customer experience.

4. Cybersecurity Specialists: Protecting AI Systems

As AI becomes more prevalent, protecting these systems from cyber threats is critical. Cybersecurity specialists focus on securing AI algorithms, data, and infrastructure from attacks.

Key Responsibilities:

- Identifying vulnerabilities in AI systems and implementing safeguards.
- Monitoring AI operations to detect and respond to cyberattacks.
- Ensuring compliance with data privacy and security regulations.

Example in Practice:

A cybersecurity specialist working for a financial institution might protect an AI-powered fraud detection system from hackers attempting to manipulate transaction data.

5. Data Curators: Ensuring High-Quality Inputs

AI systems are only as good as the data they are trained on. Data curators ensure that AI systems receive accurate, relevant, and unbiased data, enabling them to function effectively.

Key Responsibilities:

- Cleaning and organizing raw data for use in AI training.
- Identifying and addressing bias in datasets.
- Updating datasets to reflect changing conditions or trends.

Example in Practice:

A data curator at an e-commerce platform might refine product recommendation algorithms by removing outdated or irrelevant data from the training set.

6. Sustainability Analysts: Leveraging AI for Environmental Goals

As organizations focus on sustainability, AI is playing a key role in addressing environmental challenges. Sustainability analysts use AI tools to monitor energy consumption, reduce waste, and model the impact of climate policies.

Key Responsibilities:

- Analyzing environmental data to identify patterns and trends.
- Using AI to optimize resource use, such as energy or water.
- Developing AI-driven solutions for renewable energy, carbon capture, or waste management.

Example in Practice:

A sustainability analyst at a renewable energy company might use AI to predict demand fluctuations and optimize the operation of solar farms.

7. AI Integration Specialists: Bridging Technology and Business

AI integration specialists ensure that AI solutions are effectively implemented across organizations, delivering value while minimizing disruption.

Key Responsibilities:

- Identifying use cases for AI within a business.
- Managing the deployment of AI tools and systems.
- Training employees to use AI technologies effectively.

Example in Practice:

An AI integration specialist at a retail company might oversee the rollout of a predictive analytics system that forecasts inventory needs, training store managers to interpret and act on AI-generated insights.

Preparing for the Future

The transformation of the labor market presents both challenges and opportunities. To thrive in this new world of work, individuals, businesses, and governments must embrace adaptability, continuous learning, and collaboration.

For Workers

- Focus on developing skills that complement AI, such as creativity, critical thinking, and emotional intelligence.
- Pursue lifelong learning through online courses, vocational training, and on-the-job experiences.
- Stay informed about emerging trends and industries to identify new opportunities.

For Businesses

- Invest in reskilling and upskilling programs to prepare employees for AI-enhanced roles.
- Foster a culture of innovation and adaptability, encouraging workers to embrace new technologies.
- Prioritize ethical AI practices and ensure transparency in decision-making.

For Governments

- Fund education and workforce development initiatives to address the skills gap.
- Create policies that support workers during transitions, such as unemployment benefits or wage subsidies.
- Collaborate with industry leaders to develop ethical guidelines and standards for AI use.

Conclusion: Navigating the New World of Work

The rise of AI is reshaping the labor market in profound and unpredictable ways. While some jobs will change and others will grow, the consistent theme is transformation. Understanding these shifts – and preparing for them—will be essential for workers, businesses, and governments alike.

In the AI-driven economy, adaptability and lifelong learning will be the keys to staying relevant. By embracing the opportunities of AI and navigating its challenges responsibly, we can create a future where technology enhances human potential rather than diminishing it. The labor market of tomorrow is one of growth, innovation, and collaboration—and it is ours to shape.

Chapter 16
The Agent Manager Role

As AI systems increasingly take on routine, repetitive, and rules-based tasks, the human role in the workforce is undergoing a significant evolution. Rather than being replaced by automation, many workers will transition to roles that involve overseeing, optimizing, and collaborating with AI systems to meet organizational objectives. At the heart of this transformation is the rise of the **Agent Manager**—a new position that blends technical expertise, strategic decision-making, and emotional intelligence.

The **Agent Manager** will be a linchpin of the AI-driven workplace, serving as the critical human link between AI agents and organizational goals. This chapter delves into the responsibilities, skills, and future significance of this emerging role, exploring how it will shape the future of work.

What is an Agent Manager?

The term "agent manager" refers to a professional tasked with managing AI agents—intelligent systems designed to perform specific tasks, such as customer support, data analysis, fraud detection, or supply chain optimization. Unlike traditional managers, who oversee human teams, agent managers work with AI systems to ensure they are functioning effectively, making decisions aligned with organizational values, and adapting to changing conditions.

In essence, the agent manager is not just a supervisor but a collaborator, working alongside AI to enhance performance, solve problems, and provide the human judgment that AI inherently lacks.

Core Responsibilities of an Agent Manager

The agent manager role is multifaceted, requiring a combination of technical, analytical, and interpersonal skills. Below are the key responsibilities that define the role:

1. Decision Oversight

AI agents excel at making recommendations and predictions based on data, but they are not infallible. An agent manager's primary responsibility is to review and refine the decisions made by AI systems to ensure they align with organizational objectives and ethical standards.

- **Example**: In a financial institution, an AI fraud detection system might flag unusual transactions. The agent manager would review these alerts, determine their validity, and decide whether to escalate the issue or override the AI's recommendation.
- **Key Tasks**:
    - Assessing the accuracy and relevance of AI outputs.
    - Balancing AI-driven recommendations with human judgment.
    - Making final decisions in ambiguous or high-stakes scenarios.

2. Training AI Agents

AI systems are not static; they require continuous learning and updates to remain effective. Agent managers play a critical role in training AI agents by providing them with new data, rules, and parameters. Additionally, they help fine-tune AI systems to adapt to evolving business needs and address errors or biases in their decision-making processes.

- **Example**: In an e-commerce company, an AI recommendation engine might need to be updated to account for new product categories or customer behavior trends. The agent manager would curate relevant data and adjust the system's algorithms accordingly.

- **Key Tasks:**
  - Feeding AI systems with high-quality, labeled data.
  - Updating rules and parameters to reflect changing organizational priorities.
  - Identifying and correcting biases in AI outputs.

3. Problem-Solving

While AI agents are highly effective at handling routine tasks, they often struggle with complex, nuanced, or unexpected problems. Agent managers step in to address these situations, providing the empathy, creativity, and ethical consideration that AI cannot replicate.

- **Example**: In healthcare, an AI system might recommend a particular treatment based on patient data. However, if the patient has unique circumstances (e.g., cultural preferences or rare comorbidities), the agent manager—a doctor or healthcare professional—would adjust the recommendation accordingly.
- **Key Tasks**:
  - Resolving ethical dilemmas or conflicts that AI systems cannot navigate.
  - Managing edge cases or scenarios that fall outside the AI's programmed capabilities.
  - Intervening in situations requiring personal interaction or emotional sensitivity.

4. Monitoring Performance

AI systems are not immune to errors, biases, or degradation over time. Agent managers are responsible for tracking the performance of AI agents to ensure they remain accurate, efficient, and reliable. This involves setting key performance indicators (KPIs), analyzing system outputs, and conducting regular audits.

- **Example**: In a logistics company, an AI-powered route optimization system might be monitored to ensure it consistently reduces delivery times and fuel consumption. If the system starts underperforming, the agent manager investigates and makes adjustments.
- **Key Tasks**:
    - Establishing metrics to evaluate AI performance (e.g., accuracy, speed, user satisfaction).
    - Detecting anomalies or declines in system performance.
    - Coordinating with technical teams to address technical issues or implement upgrades.

Skills of an Effective Agent Manager

The agent manager role combines elements of technical expertise, strategic thinking, and interpersonal skills. Below are the core competencies required for success in this role:

1. Analytical Thinking

Agent managers must be able to interpret AI outputs, assess their relevance, and make informed decisions based on data. This requires strong analytical skills, as well as the ability to weigh multiple factors and anticipate potential outcomes.

- **Why It Matters**: AI systems often generate vast amounts of data and complex recommendations. Agent managers must cut through the noise to identify actionable insights.
- **Example**: A retail agent manager might analyze AI-generated sales forecasts to identify trends and adjust inventory levels accordingly.

2. Technical Literacy

While agent managers are not required to be AI engineers, they must have a basic understanding of how AI systems work, their capabilities, and their limitations. This technical literacy enables them to collaborate effectively with data scientists and software developers.

- **Why It Matters**: Understanding the "why" behind AI decisions allows agent managers to identify errors, biases, or areas for improvement.
- **Example**: An agent manager in a marketing firm might need to understand how an AI algorithm ranks customer leads to ensure it aligns with the company's sales strategy.

3. Emotional Intelligence

AI systems lack the ability to understand human emotions or navigate sensitive interpersonal situations. Agent managers must fill this gap by demonstrating empathy, emotional intelligence, and cultural awareness.

- **Why It Matters**: Many decisions require a human touch, particularly in industries like healthcare, customer service, and education.
- **Example**: A customer service agent manager might need to intervene when an AI chatbot fails to resolve a frustrated customer's issue, ensuring the customer feels heard and valued.

4. Leadership and Collaboration

Agent managers work at the intersection of humans and machines, requiring strong leadership skills to align teams around shared goals. Additionally, they must collaborate effectively with technical teams, business leaders, and end-users.

- **Why It Matters**: Effective leadership ensures that AI systems are used in ways that benefit both the organization and its employees.

- **Example**: An agent manager in a manufacturing plant might lead a cross-functional team to integrate AI-powered predictive maintenance tools into daily operations.

5. Ethics and Responsibility

As the stewards of AI systems, agent managers are responsible for ensuring that these tools are used ethically and transparently. This requires a strong moral compass and a commitment to fairness, accountability, and inclusivity.

- **Why It Matters**: AI systems can unintentionally perpetuate biases or make decisions that conflict with societal norms. Agent managers must act as gatekeepers to prevent such outcomes.
- **Example**: In a hiring context, an agent manager might review AI-driven candidate screening processes to ensure they do not discriminate based on race, gender, or age.

The Agent Manager as a Cornerstone of the Future Workforce

The rise of the agent manager role signals a broader shift in the nature of work. By 2030, it is expected that most organizations will rely heavily on AI systems to drive efficiency, innovation, and decision-making. However, the success of these systems will depend on the human professionals who oversee and guide them.

The agent manager role represents a hybrid of technical expertise and leadership, making it a cornerstone of the future workforce. Below are some of the ways in which this role will shape the future of work:

1. Bridging the Human-Machine Divide

Agent managers will serve as the critical link between AI systems and human workers, ensuring that machines enhance—not replace—human capabilities. By fostering collaboration between humans and AI, these professionals will create more productive and harmonious workplaces.

2. Driving Ethical and Responsible AI Adoption

As organizations deploy increasingly powerful AI systems, agent managers will play a key role in ensuring that these tools are used ethically and responsibly. By prioritizing transparency, accountability, and fairness, they will help build trust in AI technologies.

3. Enabling Organizational Agility

In a rapidly changing business environment, agent managers will help organizations adapt to new challenges and opportunities. Their ability to oversee, optimize, and innovate with AI systems will enable companies to respond quickly to market shifts, technological advancements, and customer needs.

4. Creating a New Class of Jobs

The agent manager role is just one example of how AI is creating entirely new professions. As the AI economy matures, additional roles will emerge, requiring a combination of human creativity, technical expertise, and emotional intelligence.

Preparing for the Agent Manager Role

For workers aspiring to become agent managers, preparation is key. Below are actionable steps for building the skills and experience needed for this role:

- **Learn the Basics of AI**: Take online courses or attend workshops on AI fundamentals, such as machine learning, data analysis, and natural language processing.
- **Develop Analytical Skills**: Practice interpreting data, identifying patterns, and making evidence-based decisions.
- **Focus on Emotional Intelligence**: Work on communication, empathy, and conflict resolution skills to handle human-centric challenges.

- **Gain Industry Experience**: Build expertise in a specific industry, whether it's healthcare, finance, retail, or manufacturing, to understand its unique challenges and opportunities.
- **Stay Informed**: Keep up with the latest developments in AI technology, ethics, and regulation to remain relevant in a rapidly evolving field.

Conclusion: Embracing the Future of Work

The advent of AI is not a story of replacement, but of transformation. The agent manager role exemplifies this shift, blending the best of human and machine capabilities to drive innovation, solve problems, and achieve organizational goals. As this role becomes a cornerstone of the future workforce, it will redefine what it means to work in an AI-driven world.

By embracing adaptability, lifelong learning, and ethical responsibility, agent managers will not only thrive in the new labor market but also help shape a future where humans and AI work together to create value, solve problems, and make the world a better place.

Chapter 17
Building an Agent-Ready Organization

The rise of artificial intelligence (AI) is not just reshaping the labor market—it is redefining the very fabric of how businesses operate. To thrive in an AI-driven economy, organizations must become **agent-ready**, meaning they must rethink their workflows, organizational culture, and infrastructure to fully integrate AI agents into their operations. This transformation goes beyond adopting new technologies; it requires a holistic approach that aligns people, processes, and systems around AI's capabilities.

Becoming agent-ready is not merely a competitive advantage—it is an imperative for survival in the rapidly evolving business landscape. This chapter outlines the key steps organizations must take to build an agent-ready workforce, foster collaboration between humans and AI, and position themselves as leaders in the new labor market.

Key Steps to Build an Agent-Ready Organization

Organizations that aim to leverage AI effectively must address four critical areas: redesigning workflows, fostering a culture of collaboration, investing in infrastructure, and upskilling the workforce. Each of these steps plays a vital role in creating an environment where humans and AI can work together seamlessly.

1. Redesign Workflows

The integration of AI into organizational workflows is not about replacing humans but about **augmenting human capabilities**. To achieve this, organizations must identify tasks that can be automated and restructure roles to focus on activities where human judgment, creativity, and empathy are essential.

Key Actions:

- **Identify Tasks Suitable for Automation:** Begin by analyzing existing workflows to identify repetitive, rules-based tasks that can be handled by AI agents. Examples include data entry, scheduling, invoice processing, and routine customer queries. **Example:** A retail company might automate inventory tracking using AI while reallocating human workers to focus on customer engagement and personalized sales strategies.
- **Restructure Roles Around High-Value Activities:** Once routine tasks are automated, redefine roles to emphasize higher-value activities such as strategy, innovation, and problem-solving. **Example:** In a logistics company, warehouse staff might transition from manual sorting to overseeing and maintaining AI-powered robots that handle inventory.
- **Create Clear Human-AI Interfaces:** Design workflows and interfaces that enable humans and AI agents to collaborate seamlessly. This includes:
  - Dashboards where employees can review and refine AI-generated recommendations.
  - Tools that allow for easy escalation of complex issues from AI agents to human managers.

    Example: In a customer service setting, an AI chatbot might handle routine inquiries but transfer complicated or emotionally sensitive cases to a human agent.

2. Develop a Culture of Collaboration

AI adoption is as much about mindset as it is about technology. To become agent-ready, organizations must foster a culture where

employees view AI as a **partner** rather than a competitor. Building trust in AI systems and encouraging collaboration between humans and machines are critical to this cultural shift.

Key Actions:

- **Promote AI as a Partner:** Help employees understand that AI is not here to replace their roles but to enhance their productivity and creativity. Highlight how AI can take over mundane tasks, allowing workers to focus on more meaningful and rewarding activities.
  Example: A marketing team might use AI to analyze campaign performance, freeing up team members to brainstorm creative strategies.
- **Foster Trust Through Transparency:** Employees are more likely to embrace AI if they understand how it works. Organizations should:
  - Explain the logic behind AI decisions.
  - Provide transparency about data usage and system limitations.
    Example: A financial services firm might hold workshops to demonstrate how its AI-powered fraud detection system identifies suspicious transactions.
- **Provide Training to Build Confidence:** Offer training sessions to familiarize employees with AI tools and systems. This reduces fear and resistance while empowering workers to collaborate effectively with AI.

  Example: A healthcare organization might train nurses to use AI-powered patient monitoring tools, helping them interpret data and respond to alerts.

3. Invest in Infrastructure

Becoming agent-ready requires robust infrastructure that enables the smooth integration of AI agents across departments. This includes adopting the right tools, platforms, and security measures to support AI-driven operations.

Key Actions:

- **Adopt AI-Ready Tools and Platforms:** Invest in software and hardware solutions that allow AI systems to integrate seamlessly with existing workflows and databases. Look for platforms that are scalable, customizable, and user-friendly.

  Example: A manufacturing company might implement an AI-powered enterprise resource planning (ERP) system to streamline supply chain operations.
- **Ensure Cybersecurity and Data Privacy:** Protecting AI systems and their outputs from cyberattacks is critical. Organizations must:
  - Secure the data used to train AI models.
  - Monitor AI systems for vulnerabilities.

    Example: A bank using AI for credit risk assessment must ensure its models are protected against data breaches and adversarial attacks.
- **Leverage Cloud and Edge Computing:** Cloud computing provides the scalability needed for AI training and deployment, while edge computing enables real-time AI processing at the source (e.g., IoT devices).

  Example: A transportation company might use edge computing to power AI systems in autonomous vehicles, allowing them to process data locally for faster decision-making.

4. Upskill the Workforce

AI's integration into the workplace demands a workforce that is not only familiar with AI tools but also capable of adapting to new roles and responsibilities. Upskilling employees is essential to building an agent-ready organization.

Key Actions:

- **Offer Training Programs for AI-Aligned Roles:** Provide employees with opportunities to learn the skills needed for roles such as agent managers, data curators, and AI trainers. Training programs can include:
    - Online courses on AI fundamentals.
    - In-house workshops on specific tools and systems.
    - Partnerships with educational institutions for certification programs.

      Example: A retail chain might train store managers to use AI-powered demand forecasting tools, enabling them to make data-driven decisions.
- **Encourage Lifelong Learning:** Foster a culture of continuous learning by incentivizing employees to update their skills regularly.

  Example: A technology company might offer employees a stipend to enroll in AI-related courses on platforms like Coursera or Udemy.
- **Reskill Displaced Workers:** For employees whose roles are being automated, provide reskilling opportunities to help them transition into new positions within the organization.

  Example: A logistics company might train warehouse workers to become drone operators or supervisors of automated systems.

5. Foster Cross-Functional Teams

AI adoption is not solely a technical endeavor—it requires collaboration between technical experts, domain specialists, and ethics officers to ensure that AI implementations align with business goals and societal values. Cross-functional teams are essential for successful AI integration.

Key Actions:

- **Combine Diverse Skill Sets:** Build teams that include:
    - AI developers who design and optimize algorithms.
    - Domain experts who understand industry-specific challenges.
    - Ethics officers who ensure AI systems align with organizational values.

    Example: A healthcare organization implementing an AI diagnostic tool might assemble a team comprising software engineers, physicians, and patient advocates.
- **Encourage Interdisciplinary Collaboration:** Create opportunities for team members from different disciplines to share knowledge and perspectives.

  Example: In a media company, content creators and data scientists might collaborate to develop AI tools that personalize user experiences.
- **Establish Clear Goals and Metrics:** Define success metrics that reflect both technical performance and broader organizational objectives.

  Example: An AI implementation team in a retail company might measure success based on both customer satisfaction and revenue growth.

Benefits of Building an Agent-Ready Organization

Organizations that embrace these changes will unlock significant benefits, positioning themselves as leaders in the AI-driven economy. Key advantages include:

1. **Increased Productivity**: Automating routine tasks allows employees to focus on high-value activities, boosting organizational efficiency.
2. **Enhanced Innovation**: AI provides insights and capabilities that enable organizations to develop new products, services, and business models.
3. **Improved Employee Satisfaction**: By offloading mundane tasks to AI, workers can engage in more meaningful and fulfilling roles.
4. **Stronger Competitive Advantage**: Companies that integrate AI effectively will gain a significant edge in their industries, staying ahead of competitors that lag in adoption.
5. **Resilience to Market Changes**: AI-driven organizations are better equipped to adapt to economic shifts, technological advancements, and customer demands.

Case Study: A Retail Giant Becomes Agent-Ready

Consider the transformation of a global retail giant that adopted AI to streamline operations and enhance customer experiences. Here's how the company became agent-ready:

- **Redesigned Workflows**: Automated inventory management reduced stockouts and overstocking, while store employees focused on personalized customer service.
- **Developed a Culture of Collaboration**: Workshops and training sessions helped employees embrace AI as a partner, improving adoption rates.

- **Invested in Infrastructure**: The company implemented an AI-powered ERP system that integrated inventory, sales, and supply chain data across all locations.
- **Upskilled the Workforce**: Store managers were trained to use AI tools to analyze sales trends and optimize product placement.
- **Fostered Cross-Functional Teams**: AI developers worked alongside retail specialists to create tools tailored to the company's unique challenges.

As a result, the company saw a 20% increase in operational efficiency, a 15% boost in customer satisfaction, and a significant reduction in inventory costs.

Conclusion: The Path to an Agent-Ready Future

Building an agent-ready organization is not a one-time initiative—it is an ongoing journey that requires commitment, adaptability, and collaboration. By redesigning workflows, fostering a culture of collaboration, investing in infrastructure, upskilling the workforce, and assembling cross-functional teams, organizations can position themselves to thrive in the AI-driven economy.

The future belongs to businesses that embrace AI as an enabler of human potential, not a replacement for it. By becoming agent-ready, organizations will not only increase productivity and innovation but also create workplaces where humans and machines work together to achieve extraordinary results. This transformation is not just about surviving the future of work—it's about leading it.

Chapter 18
Incentives, Productivity, and Measurement

Artificial intelligence (AI) is revolutionizing how organizations operate, driving innovation, efficiency, and decision-making. However, to fully harness the potential of AI, organizations must rethink traditional frameworks for productivity, incentives, and performance measurement. The integration of AI into the workforce challenges long-established norms, such as measuring success by hours worked or tasks completed, and necessitates a more nuanced approach to evaluating human and machine contributions.

This chapter explores how organizations can redefine productivity metrics, design effective incentive structures, and balance the roles of AI and human workers in a way that fosters trust, collaboration, and innovation.

Rethinking Productivity

Traditional productivity metrics, such as output volume, hours worked, or the speed of task completion, were developed in an era of human-dominated workforces. However, these metrics often fail to capture the value generated in an AI-augmented workplace, where much of the "output" may come from machines rather than humans. To adapt, organizations must shift toward measuring outcomes, collaboration, and innovation.

1. From Raw Output to Outcome-Based Metrics

In an AI-driven environment, success should not be measured by the quantity of tasks completed but by the quality of decisions, innovations, and outcomes. This shift aligns productivity metrics with the broader goals of the organization.

- **Focus on Results, Not Processes**: Measure the impact of work, such as customer satisfaction, revenue growth, or problem resolution, rather than the number of tasks performed.

  Example: In customer service, instead of tracking the number of calls handled, measure customer retention, issue resolution rates, or Net Promoter Scores (NPS).

- **Value Creation**: Highlight metrics that reflect value delivered to stakeholders, such as time saved, costs reduced, or innovations introduced.
  Example: A healthcare provider using AI for diagnostics might track metrics like early disease detection rates or improved patient outcomes instead of the number of tests conducted.

2. Collaboration Metrics: Human and AI Synergy

In the AI-augmented workforce, productivity depends on how effectively humans and AI systems work together. Collaboration metrics help organizations evaluate the success of these partnerships.

- **Human-AI Workflows**: Assess how well AI systems integrate into human workflows. Metrics could include the accuracy of AI recommendations and the speed at which humans act on them.
  Example: In retail, measure how effectively AI-powered inventory tools support human managers in reducing stockouts and overstock.

- **Adoption and Utilization Rates**: Track how frequently employees use AI tools and whether they trust the outputs. High adoption rates reflect effective integration.

Example: In marketing, measure how often teams rely on AI tools for customer segmentation or campaign optimization.

3. Metrics for Innovation

AI has the potential to unlock creativity and innovation by automating routine tasks. Organizations should evaluate the extent to which AI enables new ideas, products, or business models.

- **Rate of Innovation**: Measure the number of new ideas generated, patents filed, or products launched with the support of AI. **Example**: A manufacturing company might track how AI-driven predictive analytics leads to process improvements or cost reductions.
- **Experimentation Success Rates**: Use metrics to assess how AI enables teams to test and implement new approaches. **Example**: In financial services, measure how AI-powered simulations help teams refine investment strategies.

Incentivizing the Workforce

As AI reshapes workflows, organizations must rethink how they motivate and reward employees. Effective incentive systems should reflect the evolving roles of workers and encourage behaviors that align with organizational goals in an AI-driven world.

1. Performance-Based Rewards

Traditional performance metrics often fail to account for AI's contributions. Organizations should align rewards with outcomes that reflect both individual contributions and AI-driven enhancements.

- **Outcome-Oriented Incentives**: Reward employees based on measurable results, such as increased efficiency, improved customer satisfaction, or successful AI integration.

Example: A logistics manager might receive bonuses tied to improvements in delivery times achieved through AI-optimized routing.

- **AI Collaboration Metrics**: Recognize employees who effectively collaborate with AI systems, such as those who improve AI performance through training or creative problem-solving.

  Example: A fraud analyst who refines AI algorithms to identify new fraud patterns might earn recognition for their contributions.

2. Learning Incentives

In an AI-driven economy, continuous learning is essential for staying relevant. Organizations should incentivize employees to acquire new skills and certifications related to AI.

- **Skill-Based Rewards**: Provide financial rewards, promotions, or recognition to employees who complete training programs or earn certifications in AI-related fields.

  Example: A marketing professional who learns to use AI-driven analytics tools might qualify for a salary increase or a new role.

- **Gamified Learning Incentives**: Use gamification to encourage participation in training programs, offering points, badges, or rewards for completing learning milestones.

  Example: A sales team might compete to earn the highest scores in an AI training module, with top performers receiving bonuses or recognition.

3. Team-Based Rewards

AI often enhances productivity at the team level, making it essential to incentivize collaboration rather than individual performance alone.

- **Shared Success Metrics**: Reward teams that demonstrate effective integration of AI into their workflows and achieve collective goals.

Example: A product development team might receive bonuses for successfully launching an AI-enhanced product ahead of schedule.

- **Cross-Functional Collaboration**: Incentivize teams that bring together diverse expertise, such as technical experts, domain specialists, and ethics officers, to implement AI solutions. **Example**: A cross-functional team designing an AI-powered customer service solution might be rewarded for achieving high customer satisfaction scores.

Balancing AI and Human Contributions

While AI enhances productivity, its growing role in the workforce can create challenges related to trust, morale, and employee empowerment. Organizations must ensure that workers feel valued and empowered, even as AI takes on more responsibilities.

1. Clear Communication About AI Roles

Transparency is key to building trust and maintaining morale. Employees need to understand what AI can—and cannot—do, as well as how it complements their roles.

- **Define AI's Limits**: Clearly communicate the tasks AI is designed to handle and emphasize that human judgment remains essential in many areas.

  Example: In finance, employees should know that while AI can analyze market trends, humans make the final investment decisions.

- **Highlight Human Value**: Reinforce the unique contributions humans bring to the table, such as creativity, empathy, and ethical decision-making.

  Example: A healthcare organization might emphasize that while AI assists in diagnostics, doctors provide the personal care and context-sensitive recommendations patients need.

2. Involve Employees in AI Implementation

Workers are more likely to embrace AI if they have a voice in its development and deployment.

- **Co-Design AI Systems**: Engage employees in the design and testing of AI tools to ensure they meet user needs and align with workflows.

  Example: A customer service team might provide feedback on the design of an AI chatbot to ensure it reflects real-world customer interactions.

- **Solicit Feedback Regularly**: Create channels for employees to share their experiences with AI tools and suggest improvements. **Example**: A retail company might hold monthly forums where store managers discuss how AI-driven inventory systems are performing.

3. Celebrate Human-AI Collaboration

Recognize and celebrate examples of successful collaboration between humans and AI.

- **Case Studies and Success Stories**: Share stories of how employees have used AI to achieve outstanding results, inspiring others to embrace the technology.

  Example: A logistics company might highlight how an operations manager used AI to reduce delivery delays during a peak season.

- **Awards for Collaboration**: Create awards or recognition programs for teams or individuals who exemplify effective human-AI collaboration.

  Example: A company might introduce an "AI Innovator of the Year" award to celebrate employees who creatively leverage AI tools.

Looking Ahead: Redefining Success in the AI Economy

By rethinking productivity metrics, designing effective incentives, and fostering a culture of collaboration, organizations can unlock the full potential of AI while empowering their workforce. The transition to an AI-integrated economy is not without challenges, but it provides an opportunity to create more meaningful, innovative, and fulfilling workplaces.

Chapter 20: Education, Training, and Credentialing

As artificial intelligence reshapes the labor market, education and training systems must adapt to prepare workers for new roles and responsibilities. The traditional model of education—where individuals complete their formal schooling early in life and rely on those skills for decades—is increasingly inadequate in an AI-driven world. Instead, lifelong learning, micro-credentialing, and AI literacy will be essential for workers to remain competitive and thrive.

This chapter explores how education, training, and credentialing systems can evolve to meet the demands of the AI economy.

Revolutionizing Education

To prepare future generations for an AI-integrated workforce, education systems must evolve to emphasize both technical skills and human capabilities.

1. AI Literacy for All

Understanding AI is no longer optional—it is a fundamental skill for navigating the modern world. Schools must introduce AI basics into their curricula to ensure that all students, regardless of career path, can engage with AI systems.

- **Core Topics**: AI fundamentals, data literacy, machine learning basics, and ethical considerations.

Example: High school students might learn how AI algorithms power social media platforms or recommendation systems.

- **Hands-On Learning**: Incorporate practical exercises, such as programming simple AI models or exploring real-world AI applications.

  Example: A middle school class might use tools like Scratch or Python to program chatbots.

2. Focus on Human Skills

While AI excels at tasks requiring logic and pattern recognition, it cannot replicate uniquely human skills such as creativity, critical thinking, and emotional intelligence.

- **Creativity and Problem-Solving**: Encourage students to approach problems from multiple perspectives and develop innovative solutions.

  Example: A design class might challenge students to create AI-powered products that address social or environmental issues.

- **Ethics and Empathy**: Teach students to consider the societal impact of AI technologies and make decisions that prioritize fairness and inclusivity.

  Example: A philosophy class might explore the ethical dilemmas posed by autonomous vehicles.

Part V: Ethics, Governance, and Society

The rise of artificial intelligence (AI) is transforming economies, industries, and workplaces, but its impact extends far beyond technology and productivity. AI is reshaping the foundational principles of society, raising profound ethical questions, challenging existing governance frameworks, and influencing how people interact with each other and their institutions. As AI becomes more pervasive, the need to address its broader implications has never been more urgent.

This section explores the ethical dilemmas posed by AI, the governance structures required to ensure its responsible use, and the societal shifts that accompany its adoption. By examining these themes, we aim to provide a roadmap for navigating the challenges and opportunities of an AI-driven world.

Chapter 19
Safety by Design

As artificial intelligence (AI) becomes an integral part of society, ensuring its safety is no longer optional—it is a necessity. AI systems now influence decisions in healthcare, finance, defense, transportation, and countless other sectors, where mistakes or failures can have catastrophic consequences. The risks range from unintended consequences and biases to malicious misuse and systemic failures. To address these challenges, **safety must be prioritized by design**, incorporated into every phase of AI development and deployment, rather than being treated as an afterthought.

This chapter explores the principles and practices of "Safety by Design," detailing how organizations, developers, and regulators can embed safety into AI systems from conception to deployment. By adopting these measures, we can mitigate risks while maximizing the transformative potential of AI.

Why Safety by Design Matters

AI systems are unlike traditional software. Their complexity, reliance on vast datasets, and ability to evolve through machine learning make them both powerful and unpredictable. Without robust safety measures, AI systems can:

1. **Make harmful decisions** due to flawed algorithms or biased training data.
2. **Fail under unexpected conditions**, causing disruption or harm.
3. **Be exploited by malicious actors** for fraud, cyberattacks, or disinformation.

4. **Erode public trust**, hindering adoption and innovation.

Safety by Design addresses these risks by ensuring that AI systems are resilient, transparent, ethical, and aligned with human values.

Key Aspects of Safety by Design

To build safe and trustworthy AI, developers and organizations must focus on the following core aspects:

1. Robust Testing

AI systems must undergo rigorous testing to ensure reliability, accuracy, and resilience. This includes simulating diverse scenarios, identifying vulnerabilities, and assessing performance under challenging conditions.

Key Approaches to Robust Testing:

- **Stress Testing**: Subject AI systems to extreme or rare scenarios to evaluate their behavior and identify weaknesses.

  Example: Testing an autonomous vehicle in heavy rain, snow, or urban environments with unpredictable pedestrian behavior.
- **Adversarial Testing**: Expose AI systems to deliberate attacks or manipulations to ensure they can withstand malicious inputs.

  Example: Testing a facial recognition system against adversarial images designed to fool it, such as altered photos or disguises.
- **Diverse Dataset Validation**: Ensure that AI systems are trained and tested on datasets representing diverse populations, environments, and use cases.

  Example: A healthcare diagnostic AI should be tested on medical data from patients of different ethnicities, ages, and genders to avoid biased results.

- **Continuous Monitoring**: AI systems should be monitored post-deployment to detect and address performance issues or vulnerabilities that emerge over time.

  Example: AI-powered fraud detection systems in banking should be regularly updated as new types of fraud are identified.

2. Fail-Safe Mechanisms

AI systems must be designed with clear fail-safe protocols that allow them to handle errors, malfunctions, or ethical dilemmas without causing harm. These mechanisms ensure that failures are contained and manageable.

Key Fail-Safe Strategies:

- **Graceful Degradation**: When an AI system encounters an error, it should reduce functionality in a controlled manner rather than failing catastrophically.

  Example: An AI-powered drone encountering a hardware malfunction should return to its base rather than crashing or continuing its mission unsafely.

- **Fallback to Human Control**: Critical AI systems should allow humans to intervene or override decisions when necessary.

  Example: In autonomous vehicles, a driver should be able to take manual control if the AI encounters a situation it cannot handle.

- **Kill Switches**: AI systems should have mechanisms to shut down safely in the event of severe malfunctions or misuse.

  Example: An industrial robot could be equipped with an emergency stop button that halts operations immediately.

- **Boundary Constraints**: Limit the actions an AI system can take to prevent it from exceeding its intended scope.

  Example: A virtual assistant should not be able to access sensitive information or perform unauthorized financial transactions.

3. Human Oversight

AI systems, especially those operating in high-stakes domains, should not make critical decisions autonomously. Human oversight ensures that AI outputs are reviewed and contextualized before actions are taken.

Key Practices for Human Oversight:

- **Human-in-the-Loop (HITL)**: Requires human approval for critical decisions made by AI systems.

  Example: In healthcare, a doctor should review and confirm AI-generated diagnoses or treatment plans before they are implemented.

- **Human-on-the-Loop (HOTL)**: Allow humans to monitor AI systems in real time and intervene if necessary.

  Example: In defense applications, operators should monitor autonomous drones and take control if they deviate from their mission parameters.

- **Human-in-Command (HIC)**: Ensure that ultimate accountability for AI decisions rests with humans, not machines.

  Example: In finance, a compliance officer should be responsible for approving AI-driven trading strategies to ensure they align with regulations.

- **Training for Human Oversight**: Provide users with the skills and knowledge needed to understand and evaluate AI outputs.

  Example: Airline pilots must be trained to interpret and override AI autopilot systems when necessary.

4. Transparent Design

Transparency is essential for building trust in AI systems and enabling external audits. Developers should document how AI systems are built, trained, and maintained, making their processes understandable to stakeholders.

Key Elements of Transparent Design:

- **Explainable AI (XAI)**: Design AI systems that can provide clear, interpretable explanations for their decisions.

  Example: A credit scoring AI should explain why a loan application was approved or denied, detailing the factors that influenced its decision.

- **Open Documentation**: Maintain detailed records of an AI system's design, training data, algorithms, and testing results.

  Example: Developers of a self-driving car should document the vehicle's sensor configurations, decision-making processes, and safety tests.

- **Third-Party Audits**: Allow external experts to review AI systems for compliance with safety, ethical, and regulatory standards.

  Example: A facial recognition company might invite independent auditors to evaluate its system for biases and privacy risks.

- **User Communication**: Clearly inform users about the capabilities, limitations, and risks of AI systems.

  Example: A smart home assistant might provide disclaimers about data collection practices and the potential for misinterpretations.

The Role of Regulation and Standards

While developers and organizations play a crucial role in ensuring AI safety, governments and regulatory bodies must establish frameworks to enforce consistent standards. These regulations should balance innovation with public safety.

1. Regulatory Frameworks

Governments should implement laws and guidelines that mandate safety by design for AI systems, particularly in high-risk domains like healthcare, finance, and defense.

- **Risk-Based Regulation**: Classify AI systems by risk level (e.g., low, medium, high), with stricter safety requirements for higher-risk applications.

  Example: The EU's proposed AI Act categorizes AI systems based on their potential impact, imposing more stringent requirements on high-risk systems like biometric identification.
- **Liability Laws**: Clearly define who is responsible for AI failures, ensuring accountability for developers, operators, and organizations.
  Example: In the case of an autonomous vehicle accident, liability laws could specify whether the manufacturer, software developer, or user is at fault.

2. Industry Standards

Industry groups and professional organizations should develop standards for AI safety, ensuring consistency across sectors.

- **ISO Standards for AI**: The International Organization for Standardization (ISO) is developing standards for AI, covering areas like risk management, transparency, and bias mitigation.
- **Sector-Specific Standards**: Industries like healthcare and aviation should establish tailored safety guidelines to address their unique challenges.

  Example: The FDA provides guidance for AI medical devices, emphasizing transparency, performance monitoring, and patient safety.

Conclusion: Building Safer AI for the Future

Safety by Design is not just a technical challenge—it is a moral and societal imperative. By embedding safety into the development process, we can deploy AI systems with confidence, knowing they are resilient, ethical, and aligned with human values.

The path forward requires collaboration among developers, organizations, regulators, and civil society. Through robust testing, fail-safe mechanisms, human oversight, and transparent design, we can build AI systems that enhance lives while minimizing risks. In doing so, we ensure that the benefits of AI are shared equitably and responsibly across society.

Chapter 20
Bias, Fairness, and Accountability

The transformative potential of artificial intelligence (AI) comes with significant ethical challenges, particularly concerning bias, fairness, and accountability. AI systems, if not carefully designed and monitored, can reflect and amplify societal inequalities, perpetuate discrimination, and reinforce structural injustices. These unintended consequences arise from biases in training data, flawed algorithms, and a lack of oversight.

Addressing these issues is not just a technical endeavor—it is a societal imperative. Ethical AI requires deliberate action, collaboration, and a commitment to ensuring that these systems benefit all individuals equitably. This chapter explores the critical components of eliminating bias, ensuring fairness, and building accountability frameworks to create truly ethical AI.

Why Bias, Fairness, and Accountability Matter

AI systems are increasingly used to make decisions that impact people's lives—decisions about hiring, lending, healthcare, policing, and more. However, these systems are not inherently neutral. They are shaped by the data they are trained on, the algorithms that power them, and the intent behind their deployment. Without careful consideration, AI can replicate harmful patterns of discrimination and inequality.

- **Bias**: Bias in AI occurs when systems produce unfair outcomes for specific groups due to imbalanced or prejudiced training data, flawed algorithms, or systemic inequities in society.
- **Fairness**: Ensuring that AI systems treat all individuals equitably and do not disproportionately benefit or harm specific groups.

- **Accountability**: Establishing clear mechanisms to trace, audit, and take responsibility for AI systems' decisions and outcomes.

By addressing these interconnected challenges, we can build AI systems that uphold societal values, foster trust, and promote inclusivity.

Eliminating Bias

Bias in AI arises from multiple sources, including flawed datasets, algorithmic design, and cultural or systemic prejudices embedded in society. Eliminating bias requires proactive efforts at every stage of AI development and deployment.

1. Diverse Training Data

AI systems are only as unbiased as the data they are trained on. If training datasets are incomplete, unrepresentative, or skewed toward certain demographics, the resulting AI models will reflect these biases.

Key Strategies:

- **Representation Across Demographics**: Ensure that datasets include diverse populations, reflecting variations in age, gender, race, ethnicity, socioeconomic status, and geographic location.

  Example: Facial recognition systems trained predominantly on light-skinned faces have shown poor performance in accurately identifying darker-skinned individuals. Diverse training datasets can address this disparity.
- **Contextual Sensitivity**: Include data that reflects cultural, regional, and situational differences to ensure AI systems perform well in diverse contexts.

  Example: A language translation AI should be trained on texts from multiple dialects, regions, and cultural contexts to avoid mistranslations.
- **Data Augmentation**: Use techniques like synthetic data generation to fill gaps in underrepresented groups or scenarios.

Example: In medical AI, synthetic patient data can be used to supplement datasets for rare diseases or underrepresented populations.

2. Algorithmic Fairness

Bias is not only a data problem—it is also an algorithmic problem. Developers must design models that account for fairness during training and decision-making.

Key Techniques:

- **Fairness-Aware Algorithms**: Incorporate fairness constraints into machine learning models to ensure they treat all groups equitably.

  Example: In hiring AI, fairness-aware algorithms can ensure that selection rates for male and female candidates are comparable, preventing gender bias.
- **Regularization for Fairness**: Adjust model parameters during training to reduce disparate impacts across groups.

  Example: Credit scoring models can be designed to minimize differences in loan approval rates between demographic groups.
- **Bias Mitigation During Preprocessing**: Identify and correct biases in datasets before training.

  Example: Removing identifying attributes like race or gender from hiring datasets to prevent them from influencing decisions.

3. Regular Audits

AI systems should undergo regular, independent audits to identify and address biases that may emerge over time.

Key Practices:

- **Bias Detection Tools**: Use automated tools to identify biases in datasets, algorithms, and outputs.

Example: Google's What-If Tool allows developers to visualize how AI models behave for different demographic groups.

- **Third-Party Audits**: Engage external experts to evaluate AI systems for bias, fairness, and ethical compliance.

  Example: A government agency might require third-party audits of AI systems used in policing to ensure they do not disproportionately target minority communities.

- **Ongoing Monitoring**: Continuously monitor AI systems post-deployment to detect and address biases that emerge as systems interact with real-world data.

  Example: Social media platforms can monitor AI-powered content moderation systems to ensure they do not disproportionately censor specific groups or viewpoints.

Ensuring Fairness

Fairness goes beyond eliminating bias—it involves designing AI systems that actively promote equitable outcomes. This requires a deep understanding of how AI impacts different populations and a commitment to inclusivity.

1. Universal Accessibility

AI systems must be designed to serve diverse populations, including marginalized and underserved communities. Accessibility should be a core consideration from the outset.

Key Strategies:

- **Inclusive Design**: Involve diverse stakeholders in the design process to ensure AI systems meet the needs of all users.

  Example: Developers of an AI-powered education platform might consult teachers, students, and parents from underserved communities to ensure it is accessible.

- **Language and Cultural Adaptation**: Ensure AI systems are available in multiple languages and tailored to different cultural contexts.

  Example: An AI-powered healthcare chatbot should be available in local languages and culturally sensitive to patients' needs.

- **Affordability**: Ensure that AI systems are affordable for low-income users or provide subsidized access.

  Example: Governments might partner with private companies to make AI-driven agricultural tools accessible to small-scale farmers.

2. Impact Assessments

Organizations must evaluate how AI systems affect different groups to ensure equitable outcomes and avoid unintended harm.

Key Practices:

- **Equity Impact Assessments**: Assess how AI systems might affect various demographic groups before deployment.

  Example: A predictive policing AI should be evaluated for its potential to disproportionately target minority communities.

- **Scenario Testing**: Simulate the impact of AI systems in diverse scenarios to identify potential risks or harms.

  Example: A hiring AI could be tested to ensure it does not favor candidates based on factors like gender or socioeconomic background.

- **Feedback Loops**: Collect user feedback to identify and address fairness concerns post-deployment.

  Example: An AI recommendation system for job seekers could allow users to report instances of perceived unfairness, enabling continuous improvement.

Accountability Frameworks

Accountability is essential to ensure that AI systems are developed and deployed responsibly. Clear frameworks are needed to trace decisions, assign responsibility, and provide redress mechanisms when harm occurs.

1. Traceability

Traceability involves maintaining a clear record of how AI systems are built, trained, and deployed, enabling accountability when mistakes or biases occur.

Key Practices:

- **Documentation**: Maintain detailed records of datasets, algorithms, and decision-making processes.

  Example: Developers of an AI-powered loan approval system might document the sources of their training data and the criteria used in the model.
- **Version Control**: Track changes to AI models over time to ensure transparency and reproducibility.

  Example: A healthcare AI system might maintain a history of updates to its diagnostic algorithms, enabling audits.
- **Decision Logs**: Record how AI systems make decisions, particularly in high-stakes contexts.

  Example: Autonomous vehicles might record sensor data and decision paths to enable investigation of accidents.

2. Legal and Ethical Responsibility

Organizations must take responsibility for the actions of their AI systems, ensuring mechanisms for redress in case of harm.

Key Principles:

- **Liability Frameworks**: Clearly define who is responsible for AI-related harm—whether it's the developer, deployer, or user.

  Example: In the case of an autonomous vehicle accident, liability might fall on the manufacturer if the failure was due to a design flaw.

- **Ethical Oversight**: Establish ethics committees to review AI projects and ensure they align with societal values.

  Example: A tech company might convene an ethics board to review the implications of using AI in surveillance.

- **Redress Mechanisms**: Provide accessible channels for individuals to report harm caused by AI systems and seek remedies.

  Example: A hiring platform could allow rejected candidates to appeal decisions and request an explanation.

Case Studies: Bias, Fairness, and Accountability in Action

1. Facial Recognition Technology

Facial recognition systems have faced criticism for their high error rates among certain demographic groups, particularly women and people of color. Companies like Microsoft and IBM have taken steps to address these biases by:

- Expanding their training datasets to include more diverse faces.
- Publishing transparency reports detailing their systems' accuracy across demographics.
- Restricting the use of facial recognition technology in surveillance applications.

2. AI in Lending

AI-powered lending platforms have been accused of perpetuating biases in credit scoring, disproportionately disadvantaging minority borrowers. To address this:

- Regulators have mandated fairness audits for lending algorithms.
- Developers have implemented fairness-aware models to reduce disparities in loan approval rates.
- Organizations have created transparency tools to explain credit decisions to applicants.

Conclusion: Building Ethical AI for All

Bias, fairness, and accountability are not just technical challenges – they are societal imperatives. Building ethical AI requires collaboration among developers, regulators, and civil society to ensure that these systems benefit everyone equitably.

By eliminating bias, ensuring fairness, and establishing robust accountability frameworks, we can create AI systems that reflect our highest values and aspirations. In doing so, we can harness the power of AI to build a more just, inclusive, and equitable future.

Chapter 21
Data Sovereignty and Privacy

As artificial intelligence (AI) becomes increasingly embedded in everyday life, its reliance on vast amounts of data raises critical questions about data sovereignty and **privacy**. The collection, storage, and use of data underpin AI's ability to make predictions, automate tasks, and innovate across industries. However, these practices also bring challenges, such as data misuse, surveillance, and loss of control over personal and national information.

Ensuring that data is handled ethically and responsibly requires addressing two intertwined concerns: data sovereignty, which deals with who controls data, and **privacy**, which focuses on protecting individuals' rights. This chapter examines the complexities of these issues, explores solutions that balance innovation with ethical considerations, and highlights the role of governments, companies, and individuals in safeguarding data sovereignty and privacy.

The Importance of Data in AI

AI systems learn and improve by analyzing enormous datasets. Whether it's customer behavior for recommendation engines, medical records for diagnostics, or satellite imagery for environmental monitoring, data is the lifeblood of AI. Without data, AI systems cannot function effectively.

However, the reliance on data creates challenges:

1. **Volume**: The sheer quantity of data collected can overwhelm traditional systems and raise storage and security concerns.
2. **Sensitivity**: Much of the data used in AI systems is personal, such as health records, financial information, and location tracking.

3. **Globalization**: Data often flows across borders, creating conflicts between local laws and international practices.

To address these challenges, organizations must adopt robust frameworks that respect both sovereignty and privacy while enabling AI innovation.

Data Sovereignty

Data sovereignty refers to the principle that data is subject to the laws and governance structures of the country in which it is generated. It ensures that nations retain control over their data, protecting it from misuse and exploitation by foreign entities.

1. Local Control of Data

Countries and regions are increasingly asserting control over data generated within their borders, recognizing it as a strategic asset akin to natural resources. Local control of data is essential for maintaining national security, protecting citizen privacy, and fostering economic growth.

Key Measures for Local Data Control:

- **Data Localization Laws**: Require organizations to store and process data within the country where it is generated.

  Example: India's proposed Data Protection Bill mandates that sensitive personal data be stored on servers located within India.

- **Digital Infrastructure Development**: Invest in local data centers and cloud infrastructure to reduce reliance on foreign providers.

  Example: Countries like Germany and France have developed the GAIA-X project, a European cloud initiative aimed at ensuring data sovereignty.

- **Regulation of Foreign Companies**: Require multinational corporations to comply with local data protection laws.

Example: China's Cybersecurity Law mandates that companies store certain types of data within China and undergo government security reviews.

2. Cross-Border Data Sharing

While local control of data is essential, global collaboration and innovation often require cross-border data flows. Striking a balance between data sovereignty and international cooperation is critical.

Key Approaches to Secure Cross-Border Data Sharing:

- **International Agreements**: Establish treaties and frameworks that govern data sharing between countries while ensuring ethical and secure practices.

  Example: The EU-U.S. Data Privacy Framework facilitates data transfers between Europe and the United States while adhering to GDPR principles.

- **Mutual Recognition**: Countries can recognize each other's data protection standards, allowing smoother data flows.

  Example: Japan has been recognized by the EU as providing "adequate protection" under GDPR, enabling free data transfers.

- **Data Trusts**: Create neutral entities to manage and oversee cross-border data sharing, ensuring compliance with privacy and sovereignty requirements.

  Example: A healthcare data trust could allow researchers from multiple countries to access anonymized medical data for collaborative research.

Privacy in the Age of AI

AI's reliance on personal data magnifies privacy concerns. Protecting individual rights requires a proactive approach to ensure that data collection, storage, and use are ethical and transparent.

1. Privacy by Design

Privacy by Design is a framework that integrates privacy considerations into the development of AI systems from the outset, rather than treating them as an afterthought. It minimizes risks while maintaining functionality.

Principles of Privacy by Design:

- **Data Minimization**: Collect only the data necessary for the system's intended purpose.

  Example: A fitness tracker should collect step counts and heart rate data but not unnecessary personal identifiers like a user's full name or address.

- **Default Privacy Settings**: Ensure that privacy-friendly settings are enabled by default, requiring users to opt in for additional data collection.

  Example: A social media platform could make profiles private by default, allowing users to choose what information to share publicly.

- **Decentralized Data Storage**: Use decentralized models, such as blockchain, to store data securely and reduce the risk of breaches.

  Example: A healthcare system could store patient records locally on blockchain-enabled devices rather than in a centralized database.

2. User Consent and Control

Empowering individuals to control how their data is used is central to protecting privacy. Consent must be informed, explicit, and revocable.

Best Practices for User Consent and Control:

- **Clear Opt-In and Opt-Out Mechanisms**: Allow users to choose whether to share their data and to withdraw consent at any time.

Example: A mobile app could provide a simple toggle to opt out of data sharing for targeted advertisements.

- **Transparent Privacy Policies**: Use plain language to explain how data will be collected, stored, and used.

  Example: Apple's App Tracking Transparency feature informs users about what data apps are tracking and allows them to block tracking.

- **Granular Permissions**: Enable users to control specific aspects of data sharing rather than providing blanket consent.

  Example: A location-based app could allow users to share their location only during active use rather than continuously.

3. Data Anonymization

Data anonymization involves removing or masking personal identifiers from datasets to protect individual privacy while maintaining the utility of the data for analysis.

Techniques for Data Anonymization:

- **Aggregation**: Combine data points into broader categories to prevent identification of individuals.

  Example: Reporting average spending patterns for a region rather than individual transaction data.

- **Pseudonymization**: Replace identifiable information with pseudonyms or codes that cannot be traced back to individuals without additional information.

  Example: Assigning unique user IDs instead of storing names or email addresses.

- **Differential Privacy**: Introduce statistical noise into datasets to obscure individual data points while preserving overall trends.

  Example: Census data can use differential privacy to protect respondents' identities while enabling demographic analysis.

Regulating Big Tech

Big Tech companies, such as Google, Amazon, Facebook, Apple, and Microsoft, hold vast amounts of personal data. Their dominance raises concerns about monopolistic practices, data misuse, and insufficient privacy protections.

1. Enforcing Data Protection Laws

Governments play a crucial role in holding Big Tech accountable through strict data protection laws and enforcement mechanisms.

Key Regulations:

- **GDPR (General Data Protection Regulation)**: The EU's GDPR sets a global benchmark for data protection, requiring companies to obtain explicit user consent, report data breaches, and respect the right to be forgotten.

  Example: Under GDPR, Google was fined €50 million for failing to provide transparent information about data usage.
- **CCPA (California Consumer Privacy Act)**: The CCPA gives California residents the right to know what data companies collect, delete their personal data, and opt out of data sales.

  Example: A company failing to comply with CCPA could face fines and lawsuits.
- **China's PIPL (Personal Information Protection Law)**: PIPL requires companies to obtain user consent for data collection and to store sensitive data locally.

2. Breaking Up Data Monopolies

Some experts argue that breaking up Big Tech monopolies could reduce their control over personal data and foster competition.

- **Decentralized Platforms**: Encourage the development of decentralized alternatives to Big Tech platforms, such as blockchain-based social networks.
- **Data Portability**: Require companies to allow users to transfer their data to competing services.

  Example: The EU's Digital Markets Act mandates data portability to reduce dependency on dominant platforms.

3. Holding Companies Accountable

Governments and civil society must ensure that companies face consequences for data breaches, misuse, or unethical practices.

- **Hefty Fines**: Impose substantial financial penalties for violations of data protection laws.

  Example: Facebook paid $5 billion in fines to the U.S. Federal Trade Commission for privacy violations.
- **Consumer Advocacy**: Empower individuals and advocacy groups to challenge unethical data practices through legal action.

  Example: Class-action lawsuits can hold companies accountable for large-scale data breaches.

Balancing Innovation with Privacy and Sovereignty

The challenge of data sovereignty and privacy lies in balancing the need for innovation with the protection of individual rights and national interests. By adopting thoughtful policies and practices, society can achieve this balance.

Recommendations for Governments

1. **Adopt Comprehensive Privacy Laws**: Implement regulations that ensure transparency, accountability, and user control over data.
2. **Foster International Collaboration**: Work with other nations to establish global frameworks for ethical data sharing.

3. **Invest in Local Infrastructure**: Build national data centers and cloud platforms to reduce reliance on foreign providers.

Recommendations for Companies

1. **Implement Privacy by Design**: Make privacy a core principle in AI system development.
2. **Engage in Transparent Practices**: Clearly communicate data collection and usage policies to users.
3. **Prioritize Ethical Data Use**: Avoid practices that exploit or harm users, even if they are technically legal.

Recommendations for Individuals

1. **Educate Yourself**: Learn about your rights under data protection laws like GDPR or CCPA.
2. **Use Privacy Tools**: Take advantage of tools that allow you to control data collection, such as browser extensions and privacy-focused apps.
3. **Advocate for Change**: Support organizations working to promote ethical data practices and hold companies accountable.

Conclusion: Building a Responsible Data Ecosystem

In the age of AI, data sovereignty and privacy are not just technical issues—they are fundamental to preserving individual freedoms, national security, and societal trust. By embedding privacy into AI design, strengthening data sovereignty, and regulating Big Tech, society can create a responsible data ecosystem that respects individual rights while enabling technological progress.

The future of AI depends on how well we navigate these challenges. By prioritizing ethical data practices, we can ensure that AI serves humanity equitably and responsibly, laying the foundation for a more just and inclusive digital future.

Chapter 22
Environmental Costs and Efficiency

The age of artificial intelligence is upon us. AI is powering breakthroughs across healthcare, transportation, finance, and entertainment, transforming the way businesses operate and how humans live. Yet, behind every groundbreaking AI system lies an inconvenient truth: AI's rapid growth comes with **significant environmental costs**. Training massive AI models, running inference at scale, and maintaining the hardware infrastructure that enables these systems all require immense computational resources, which consume vast amounts of energy and contribute to carbon emissions.

While AI is celebrated for its potential to solve some of the world's most pressing challenges, from climate modeling to renewable energy optimization, the industry itself has a growing carbon footprint that must be addressed urgently. This chapter explores the environmental toll of AI and offers pathways to a more sustainable future—one where innovation and responsibility coexist.

The Environmental Challenges of AI

The environmental costs of AI can be categorized into three primary areas: energy consumption, hardware waste, and **resource-intensive development cycles**. These challenges are byproducts of AI's reliance on computational power, large-scale data centers, and specialized hardware.

1. Energy Consumption: AI's Hidden Power Hunger

Training a state-of-the-art AI model is not just an engineering feat—it's an energy-intensive process.

- **The Scale of Energy Use**: Training a single large language model like GPT-4 can consume as much energy as powering **several households for a year**. For instance, a 2019 study estimated that training a large natural language processing (NLP) model emits around 284 tons of CO2—equivalent to the lifetime carbon footprint of five cars.
- **Inference at Scale**: Once trained, AI models require significant energy for inference—using the model to generate predictions or outputs. In applications like real-time translation, autonomous driving, and personalized recommendations, inference happens millions or even billions of times a day, contributing to AI's ongoing energy demands.
- **Data Centers**: The "brains" behind AI systems are located in vast data centers, filled with thousands of power-hungry servers running 24/7. These facilities require not only energy to process data but also cooling systems to prevent overheating, further driving up electricity usage.

2. E-Waste: The Hardware Problem

AI relies on specialized hardware like GPUs (graphics processing units), TPUs (tensor processing units), and **ASICs (application-specific integrated circuits)** to handle the computational intensity of training and inference. The rapid pace of innovation in AI renders older hardware obsolete in a matter of years, contributing to the global e-waste problem.

- **Limited Lifespan of AI Hardware**: Servers, GPUs, and chips used to train AI models often have a lifecycle of three to five years before they are replaced. Discarded hardware adds to the growing mountain of electronic waste, much of which ends up in landfills or is improperly recycled.
- **Scarce Materials**: AI hardware depends on rare earth metals, such as lithium and cobalt, which are mined under environmentally damaging and often exploitative conditions.

- **Downstream Impacts**: The production, transportation, and disposal of AI hardware come with carbon costs, exacerbating the environmental impact of AI systems.

3. The Carbon Cost of Training and Development

Developing cutting-edge AI models involves numerous iterations of experimentation, optimization, and retraining. These cycles consume significant energy resources:

- **Hyperparameter Tuning**: Training models often requires testing thousands of configurations to find the optimal setup, multiplying energy consumption.
- **Data Preprocessing**: Cleaning and preparing the massive datasets required for AI also demands significant computational power.
- **Cloud Dependencies**: Organizations often rely on cloud providers to run AI workloads, creating a layer of abstraction that makes it harder to quantify and manage energy usage directly.

Solutions for Sustainable AI

The environmental challenges posed by AI are real, but they are not insurmountable. The industry has an opportunity—and a responsibility—to minimize its environmental impact while continuing to innovate. By prioritizing efficiency, renewable energy, and **responsible hardware practices**, AI can evolve in a way that aligns with global sustainability goals.

1. Energy-Efficient Algorithms

The key to reducing AI's environmental impact lies in improving the efficiency of algorithms. Advanced techniques can help achieve the same or better performance while consuming less computational power.

Key Strategies for Algorithmic Efficiency:

- **Sparse Models**: Sparse models use fewer parameters without compromising performance, significantly reducing the computational load.

  Example: Research into sparse transformers has shown that they can perform comparably to dense models while requiring less energy to train.

- **Federated Learning**: Instead of centralizing data for training, federated learning trains models locally on edge devices, reducing the need for massive centralized computations.

  Example: Google uses federated learning for its Gboard keyboard, training models on users' devices rather than in data centers.

- **Dynamic Neural Networks**: These models adjust their complexity based on the task at hand, using less energy for simpler tasks.

  Example: A video streaming AI might use a lightweight model to recommend standard content but switch to a more complex model for personalized recommendations.

2. Green Data Centers

Data centers are a major source of AI's energy consumption, but they can be transformed into hubs of sustainability by adopting renewable energy and efficient designs.

Key Approaches for Greener Data Centers:

- **Renewable Energy Sources**: Transitioning from fossil fuels to solar, wind, or hydroelectric power can drastically reduce the carbon footprint of data centers.

  Example: Microsoft has pledged to use 100% renewable energy for its data centers by 2025.

- **Energy-Efficient Cooling**: Innovative cooling techniques, such as liquid cooling or using naturally cold environments, can reduce the energy needed to cool servers.

  Example: Facebook's data center in Luleå, Sweden, uses the region's cold climate to cool its servers.

- **AI for Energy Management**: AI can optimize the energy usage of data centers by dynamically adjusting power consumption based on demand.

  Example: Google uses AI to manage cooling systems in its data centers, reducing energy usage by 30%.

3. Model Optimization

Training large AI models can be made significantly more efficient through techniques that reduce computational requirements without sacrificing performance.

Techniques for Model Optimization:

- **Model Pruning**: Remove unnecessary parameters from neural networks to make them smaller and more efficient.

  Example: A pruned version of a neural network might achieve 95% of the original model's accuracy while using only half the computational resources.

- **Knowledge Distillation**: Transfer knowledge from a large, complex model to a smaller, lightweight model, enabling similar performance with lower energy costs.

  Example: A small chatbot model can be trained using insights from a larger, pre-trained language model.

- **Transfer Learning**: Instead of training models from scratch, reuse pre-trained models as a foundation and fine-tune them for specific tasks.

Example: A healthcare AI system might use a pre-trained image recognition model and adapt it for identifying diseases in medical scans.

4. Lifecycle Management for Hardware

The environmental impact of AI hardware can be mitigated by adopting sustainable practices for manufacturing, recycling, and repurposing equipment.

Key Practices for Hardware Sustainability:

- **Recycling and Repurposing**: Companies should partner with e-waste recycling firms to ensure that outdated hardware is properly disposed of or repurposed.

  Example: NVIDIA offers programs for refurbishing and reselling older GPUs to reduce waste.

- **Modular Design**: Build hardware that can be easily upgraded or repaired instead of replaced.

  Example: Modular AI servers allow companies to replace individual components, such as processors or memory, without discarding the entire machine.

- **Circular Economy Initiatives**: Encourage hardware manufacturers to design products with end-of-life recyclability in mind.

  Example: Tech companies could adopt leasing models where they retain ownership of hardware and are responsible for recycling it.

The Role of Policy and Regulation

While companies and researchers can drive innovation, governments and international organizations play a critical role in ensuring that AI develops sustainably.

1. Carbon Reporting Requirements

Governments can mandate that companies disclose the carbon footprint of their AI systems, creating transparency and accountability. **Example**: The EU's proposed AI Act includes provisions for environmental impact assessments of high-risk AI systems.

2. Incentives for Green AI

Provide tax breaks or subsidies for companies that adopt energy-efficient algorithms, green data centers, or sustainable hardware practices. **Example**: Renewable energy tax credits could encourage data center operators to transition to solar or wind power.

3. International Cooperation

Global agreements can set shared standards for sustainable AI development, reducing duplication of effort and encouraging innovation. **Example**: The Paris Agreement could include provisions specifically addressing the tech sector's carbon footprint.

A Path Forward: Balancing Innovation and Responsibility

AI has the power to revolutionize industries and solve societal challenges, but its environmental costs cannot be ignored. The industry must prioritize sustainability by adopting energy-efficient algorithms, optimizing models, transitioning to green data centers, and managing hardware responsibly.

Sustainability in AI is not just an ethical imperative—it's a business opportunity. Companies that lead the charge in creating sustainable AI systems will gain competitive advantages, from reduced operational costs to enhanced brand reputation. Similarly, governments that invest in green AI infrastructure will position themselves as leaders in the global tech economy.

The question is not whether AI can be sustainable—it's whether we choose to make it so. By acting now, we can ensure that the AI revolution benefits both humanity and the planet.

Chapter 23
Collective Bargains: Regulation and Standards

Artificial intelligence (AI) technology is evolving at a breakneck pace, reshaping industries, economies, and societies. But such rapid advancement comes with risks—bias, misuse, lack of transparency, and growing concerns over control and accountability. As AI systems increasingly influence critical decisions in healthcare, finance, education, and defense, the need for robust regulation and universal standards becomes not just desirable but essential.

Governments, industries, and global organizations must work together to establish regulatory frameworks and standards that guide the ethical, safe, and responsible use of AI. This chapter explores the role of regulation, the importance of global standards, and the need for collaboration between public and private sectors to ensure AI serves the collective good.

The Role of Regulation

Regulation is critical for ensuring that AI systems are developed and deployed responsibly. Without clear laws governing AI, society risks facing unbridled misuse, exacerbation of inequalities, and erosion of public trust in the technology.

1. Protecting Public Interests

One of the primary functions of regulation is to safeguard the public from harm and ensure that AI systems prioritize safety, fairness, and privacy.

- **Safety First**: Regulations can mandate rigorous testing for AI systems, particularly those used in high-stakes environments like healthcare or autonomous vehicles.

  Example: The U.S. Food and Drug Administration (FDA) regulates AI-powered medical devices, requiring them to meet safety and efficacy standards before approval.
- **Fairness and Equity**: Laws can enforce fairness in AI systems by requiring developers to address biases in algorithms. **Example**: The EU's General Data Protection Regulation (GDPR) gives individuals the right to contest decisions made by AI systems, ensuring fair treatment.
- **Privacy Protections**: Regulations can set limits on data collection and define how personal information can be used or shared, protecting individuals from surveillance and exploitation.

  Example: California's Consumer Privacy Act (CCPA) requires companies to inform users about data collection practices and gives them the right to opt out.

2. Preventing Misuse

Clear legal frameworks can deter harmful applications of AI, from malicious uses to unintended consequences in unchecked systems.

- **Combatting Deepfakes**: AI-generated deepfakes pose a threat to democracy, public trust, and personal reputations. Regulations can require labeling or watermarking of AI-generated content to distinguish it from authentic material.

  Example: China has implemented laws requiring AI-generated media to include clear disclaimers identifying it as synthetic.
- **Autonomous Weapons**: The development of AI-powered weapons raises ethical and security concerns. International agreements can prohibit the creation and use of autonomous weapons that act without human oversight.

Example: Activist groups like the Campaign to Stop Killer Robots advocate for a global ban on lethal autonomous weapons.

- **AI in Cybercrime**: Regulations can criminalize the use of AI for hacking, phishing, and other malicious activities, holding perpetrators accountable.

3. Fostering Innovation

Contrary to fears that regulation stifles innovation, clear and thoughtfully crafted rules can provide a stable environment for growth and experimentation.

- **Clarity for Developers**: Regulations can provide developers with clear boundaries, reducing uncertainty and enabling them to innovate within defined ethical and legal parameters. **Example**: The EU's proposed AI Act categorizes AI applications by risk level, providing guidance on compliance requirements without imposing blanket restrictions.
- **Encouraging Ethical Competitiveness**: Companies adhering to high ethical standards may gain a competitive edge as consumers and investors favor responsible AI practices.
- **Example**: Microsoft and Google have adopted internal AI ethics principles, enhancing their reputations as leaders in responsible innovation.
- **Incentivizing Research**: Governments can fund research into safe and sustainable AI, accelerating innovation while addressing societal concerns.

Global Standards for AI

AI's influence transcends national borders, making global standards essential for harmonizing regulations, ensuring interoperability, and addressing cross-border challenges.

1. International Collaboration

AI governance requires cooperation across countries to address shared challenges and establish common ethical principles.

- **The Role of International Organizations**: Global entities like the United Nations (UN), the Organisation for Economic Co-operation and Development (OECD), and the International Telecommunication Union (ITU) are well-positioned to lead discussions on AI ethics and governance.

  Example: The OECD's AI Principles, adopted by over 40 countries, emphasize transparency, accountability, and human-centered values.

- **Avoiding Fragmentation**: Without global standards, divergent regulations across countries could lead to trade barriers, inefficiencies, and conflicts.

  Example: Differing data privacy laws in the EU and U.S. have complicated cross-border data transfers, highlighting the need for harmonized frameworks.

- **Preventing a Global "AI Arms Race"**: Collaborative agreements can discourage nations from prioritizing competitive advantage over ethical considerations.

  Example: The UN has called for international discussions on banning lethal autonomous weapons systems to prevent an AI-driven arms race.

2. Standardized Ethics Frameworks

Universal ethical principles can guide AI development worldwide, ensuring that systems align with shared values like transparency, accountability, and equity.

Key Principles for Global AI Ethics:

- **Transparency**: AI systems should be designed to explain their decisions in ways that are understandable to humans. **Example**: Healthcare AI systems must provide clear explanations for diagnoses or treatment recommendations.
- **Accountability**: Developers, deployers, and operators of AI systems should be held accountable for their actions and the outcomes of their systems.

  Example: Companies deploying autonomous vehicles should be liable for accidents caused by AI malfunctions.
- **Equity**: AI systems should treat all groups fairly and avoid reinforcing or amplifying existing biases.

  Example: Credit-scoring algorithms must not disproportionately disadvantage minority groups.
- **Human-Centric Design**: AI systems should prioritize human well-being, ensuring that technology serves humanity rather than undermining it.

  Example: AI-powered hiring platforms should enhance, not replace, human decision-making processes.

Public and Private Sector Cooperation

Effective AI governance requires collaboration between governments, private companies, civil society, and the general public. Each stakeholder has a role to play in ensuring ethical and responsible AI use.

1. Industry Self-Regulation

While government regulations are essential, companies must also take responsibility for the ethical development and deployment of AI.

Best Practices for Industry Self-Regulation:

- **Adopting Ethical Guidelines**: Companies can establish internal AI ethics frameworks that go beyond legal requirements.

  Example: Google's AI Principles commit the company to avoiding applications that cause harm, such as designing AI for surveillance or autonomous weapons.
- **Diversity in AI Teams**: Ensuring diverse representation in AI development teams can help address biases and create systems that reflect a broader range of perspectives.

  Example: Diverse teams are more likely to identify and address unintended consequences in AI applications.
- **Voluntary Impact Assessments**: Conducting internal audits of AI systems to evaluate their societal and environmental impacts.

  Example: A company deploying an AI-driven hiring platform might assess how its system affects different demographic groups.
- **Transparency Reports**: Companies can publish detailed reports on their AI systems, including training data, decision-making processes, and performance metrics.

  Example: OpenAI regularly publishes papers and blogs detailing the capabilities, limitations, and risks of its models.

2. Public Involvement

Policymakers must engage with communities to ensure that regulations reflect societal values and address public concerns.

Key Strategies for Public Engagement:

- **Citizen Assemblies**: Convene diverse groups of citizens to discuss the ethical implications of AI and provide input on regulatory priorities.

Example: Ireland's Citizens' Assembly on climate change could serve as a model for engaging the public on AI governance.

- **Education and Awareness**: Equip the public with knowledge about AI's benefits, risks, and ethical considerations.

  Example: Public awareness campaigns could explain how AI systems make decisions and how individuals can safeguard their data privacy.

- **Participatory Policy Development**: Involve civil society organizations, advocacy groups, and underrepresented communities in policymaking processes.

  Example: Engaging disability advocacy groups in the design of AI accessibility standards ensures inclusivity.

3. The Role of Civil Society

Non-governmental organizations (NGOs), academic institutions, and advocacy groups can play a critical role in holding governments and companies accountable.

- **Research and Advocacy**: NGOs can conduct independent research on AI's societal impacts and advocate for ethical practices.

  Example: The AI Now Institute conducts research on AI ethics and provides policy recommendations to governments and companies.

- **Public Watchdogs**: Civil society groups can monitor AI systems for misuse, bias, or adverse effects, providing a check on corporate and governmental power.

  Example: Investigative organizations can expose instances of algorithmic discrimination or unethical surveillance practices.

Case Studies in AI Regulation and Standards

1. The European Union's AI Act

The EU's proposed AI Act is one of the most comprehensive attempts at AI regulation. It categorizes AI systems based on risk levels—ranging from minimal risk (chatbots) to high risk (biometric identification) and unacceptable risk (social scoring). The Act requires stringent testing, transparency, and accountability for high-risk applications, setting a global benchmark for responsible AI governance.

2. The OECD AI Principles

Adopted by over 40 countries, the OECD AI Principles emphasize human-centered values, transparency, accountability, and inclusivity. These principles serve as a foundation for countries developing their own AI policies.

Conclusion: Harnessing AI for the Greater Good

AI has the potential to drive unparalleled progress, but its transformative power must be guided by ethical and responsible frameworks. By creating a collective bargain—through regulation, global standards, and public-private cooperation—society can harness AI's potential while minimizing its risks.

The challenge is immense, but the stakes are too high to ignore. Thoughtful governance can ensure that AI serves humanity equitably, ethically, and sustainably, paving the way for a future where technology enhances, rather than undermines, the greater good.

Part VI: AI in 2030 – Outlook and Predictions

As the world accelerates toward 2030, artificial intelligence (AI) is set to play an even more transformative role in shaping economies, societies, and individual lives. Its applications will range from solving some of humanity's most pressing problems to creating entirely new industries. However, this rapid evolution comes with challenges that must be addressed, including ethical dilemmas, economic disruptions, and geopolitical tensions. The next decade will define how AI integrates into the fabric of daily life, whether it becomes a tool for collective advancement or a force that exacerbates inequalities.

The global AI landscape by 2030 will be shaped by a mix of competition, collaboration, and regulation. The United States, China, and the European Union will remain dominant players in AI development and deployment. The United States, with its robust ecosystem of technology companies, venture capital funding, and research institutions, will continue to lead in foundational AI models and applications. China will maintain its position as a global leader in deployment, leveraging its centralized data collection infrastructure and government-driven initiatives. Meanwhile, the European Union will focus on regulated and ethical AI, crafting policies that make it a global benchmark for responsible governance. Other regions, such as India, Singapore, and parts of Africa, will emerge as centers for localized AI solutions, addressing challenges unique to their populations, such as improving healthcare access, educational quality, and agricultural efficiency.

The competition for AI dominance will intensify as nations strive to achieve technological independence. Countries will invest heavily in domestic AI ecosystems, reducing their reliance on foreign technologies for critical needs like chips, software, and cloud infrastructure. Military applications of AI will also become a focal point, with autonomous drones, cyberdefense systems, and other innovations raising ethical concerns about weaponization. Additionally, the risk of "digital colonization" will grow as developing nations rely on AI systems built by foreign companies, potentially ceding control over their data and technological sovereignty.

AI's impact will be felt across nearly every sector, but the depth of transformation will vary. In healthcare, AI will revolutionize how diseases are diagnosed and treated. Predictive healthcare systems will use AI to analyze genetic data and environmental factors, identifying diseases before symptoms even develop. Treatments will become increasingly personalized, tailored to the specific biology and medical history of individuals. Wearable devices, combined with AI-powered telemedicine platforms, will bring quality healthcare to remote and underserved regions, bridging longstanding gaps in access. By 2030, decentralized healthcare systems powered by AI could become the norm, reducing the strain on traditional medical infrastructure.

Education will also undergo a profound transformation. AI will make learning a highly personalized experience, adapting content and pace to suit each student's strengths and weaknesses. Virtual AI tutors will provide real-time feedback, helping students grasp complex concepts and improve their performance. For adults, AI-driven platforms will offer modular, on-demand courses that allow for continuous skill development, ensuring workers stay competitive in a rapidly evolving job market. AI-powered translation tools will make quality education accessible to non-English-speaking populations, breaking down barriers to knowledge and reducing global educational disparities.

The transportation sector will enter the era of autonomy by 2030, with self-driving vehicles becoming mainstream. These autonomous systems will reduce accidents, improve logistics, and lower emissions by optimizing routes and fuel consumption. Urban traffic systems will be managed by AI, dynamically adjusting signals and routes to reduce congestion. Public transportation systems will also be optimized, with AI enhancing their efficiency and sustainability. Fully autonomous delivery fleets will revolutionize supply chains, ensuring faster and more cost-effective logistics.

AI will play an essential role in combating climate change and promoting sustainability. By 2030, AI systems will be critical for predicting climate patterns and modeling the effects of rising sea levels, enabling policymakers to prepare for future risks. Renewable energy systems will benefit from AI optimization, with smarter grids balancing power supply and demand in real time. AI will also drive innovations in carbon capture technologies and sustainable agriculture, helping reduce emissions while maintaining food security. These advancements will position AI as a key tool in humanity's fight against environmental degradation.

The workplace of 2030 will be defined by collaboration between humans and AI. Machines will handle repetitive and time-intensive tasks, freeing workers to focus on creativity, strategy, and interpersonal skills. AI will act as an assistant, generating prototypes, automating administrative tasks, and providing actionable insights. While automation will displace some jobs, it will also create new roles in areas like AI maintenance, ethics oversight, and creative industries. Remote work will be further enhanced by AI-powered platforms that automate scheduling, summarize meetings, and facilitate multilingual communication.

The next decade will also see significant technological advancements in AI itself. Foundation models like GPT-4 will evolve into even more capable systems, integrating multiple modalities such as text, images, audio, and video. These multimodal systems will enable seamless interactions across formats, making AI tools more versatile. For example, a single AI system could generate lesson plans, create instructional videos, and translate them into various languages, revolutionizing how content is created and consumed. Domain-specific AI will also grow, with specialized models excelling in industries like legal research, drug discovery, and financial analysis. Transparency will become a critical focus as explainable AI systems gain prominence. These systems will come equipped with mechanisms to provide clear explanations for their decisions, ensuring trust and accountability. Human-AI interfaces will also advance, with natural language understanding reaching near-human levels. Brain-machine interfaces may emerge as early-stage tools, allowing users to control AI systems with their thoughts.

However, the promise of AI in 2030 comes with significant challenges. Ethical dilemmas will intensify as AI systems grow more powerful. Ensuring fairness in AI decision-making will remain a persistent issue, particularly as systems are deployed in sensitive areas like hiring, criminal justice, and credit scoring. Questions about autonomy versus oversight will also arise, especially in the context of autonomous vehicles and drones. Economic inequality is another pressing concern. While AI will drive productivity and innovation, it could exacerbate wealth gaps between nations and individuals. Countries with advanced AI capabilities may pull further ahead, leaving others behind. Within societies, low-skill jobs are likely to be displaced, deepening income inequality. Privacy concerns will also grow as AI systems rely on vast amounts of data. Governments and corporations may collect unprecedented levels of personal information, raising fears of surveillance and misuse.

Regulation will play a critical role in addressing these challenges, but crafting effective policies will not be easy. Governments will need to strike a balance between fostering innovation and protecting public safety. Achieving international consensus on AI governance will be particularly difficult, as nations pursue competing priorities. At the same time, overregulation could stifle innovation, limiting the potential benefits of AI and pushing innovation underground.

Despite these challenges, the vision for AI in 2030 is one of optimism and responsibility. Ethical considerations will become deeply embedded in AI development, with transparency, fairness, and accountability becoming standard practices. AI will increasingly be used to address global challenges such as poverty, inequality, and climate change, ensuring its benefits are shared equitably. Lifelong learning will extend to AI systems themselves, which will continually improve and adapt to new challenges.

By 2030, AI will not just be a tool for industry but a partner in shaping the future of humanity. The decisions we make today about regulation, collaboration, and ethical design will shape AI's trajectory in the years to come. With thoughtful planning and collective action, AI can become a force for good, driving innovation while creating a more inclusive, sustainable, and equitable world. The next decade is not just about technological progress—it is about ensuring that progress aligns with our highest values.

Chapter 24
The Ubiquity of AI

By 2030, artificial intelligence (AI) will have become a seamless and ubiquitous part of daily life, shaping how individuals interact with technology and how societies function at large. No longer confined to niche applications or specific industries, AI will be embedded into everything from personal devices to global infrastructure, quietly and efficiently influencing decisions, actions, and outcomes. With the rapid advancements in AI technologies over the past decade, the world is heading toward a future where AI is as fundamental as electricity—powering systems, enriching lives, and introducing new efficiencies. But this pervasive presence comes with profound implications, both opportunities and challenges, that must be carefully navigated to ensure this integration benefits humanity as a whole.

One of the most visible manifestations of AI's ubiquity will be in personal assistants, which by 2030 will have evolved far beyond the capabilities of current tools such as Siri, Alexa, or Google Assistant. These AI-powered companions will not only manage tasks like scheduling meetings or setting reminders but will also act as deeply personalized life managers. Equipped with advanced contextual understanding, these assistants will know their users intimately—anticipating needs, preferences, and habits. For instance, they will monitor health metrics in real time and provide actionable advice, such as suggesting dietary changes based on recent activity levels or alerting users of potential medical concerns before symptoms appear.

These AI companions will also exhibit emotional intelligence, recognizing and responding to emotional cues in conversations. They will engage in meaningful, empathetic dialogue, providing not just information but emotional support. Imagine an AI assistant that can detect stress in your voice, adjust its tone to offer reassurance, and suggest mindfulness exercises or a break from work. Such systems will not only be functional but also deeply human-like in their ability to form relational bonds with users. Leveraging real-time data from sensors, wearables, and online activities, these assistants will deliver hyper-personalized experiences, integrating seamlessly into daily routines and becoming indispensable partners in personal and professional life.

The rise of AI-powered personal assistants will be mirrored by the transformation of entire cities into smart urban ecosystems. By 2030, cities around the world will deploy AI to optimize critical infrastructure and improve quality of life for their residents. Traffic systems, for example, will be revolutionized. AI will analyze real-time data from vehicles, sensors, and cameras to dynamically adjust traffic signals, reducing congestion and minimizing travel times. Autonomous vehicles—cars, buses, and even bicycles—will dominate urban streets, offering safer, more efficient mobility options. AI-powered drones will handle last-mile deliveries, ensuring goods reach consumers quickly and sustainably. For commuters, AI systems will integrate public transit schedules with personalized navigation tools, ensuring seamless multimodal journeys.

Energy management will also be a cornerstone of AI-enabled smart cities. AI will monitor and optimize energy consumption at the municipal level, balancing supply and demand in real time. Renewable energy sources like solar and wind will be seamlessly integrated into urban grids, with AI ensuring that clean energy is stored and distributed efficiently. Public safety will be enhanced through AI-driven surveillance and predictive policing systems, which, while controversial, will be designed to preempt crimes or respond faster to emergencies. AI will also play a role in urban planning, analyzing demographic data and environmental conditions to guide sustainable development projects and optimize resource allocation.

The home will become another key domain of AI ubiquity, evolving into a fully automated, intelligent ecosystem. By 2030, AI-powered appliances and systems will anticipate user needs without requiring explicit instructions. Imagine a home where lighting and temperature adjust automatically based on your preferences and daily schedule. Refrigerators will monitor food supplies, notify you when items are running low, and place grocery orders autonomously. Washing machines will determine the optimal settings for each load based on fabric type, dirt level, and energy efficiency. Even entertainment systems will adapt to individual moods, curating playlists, shows, or reading recommendations based on real-time emotional analysis.

Interconnected AI systems will link every aspect of the home into a unified network, allowing for unparalleled convenience and efficiency. For example, a smart home might detect when you're driving home from work and begin preheating the oven for dinner, adjusting the thermostat to your preferred evening setting, and dimming the lights to create a relaxing ambiance. Voice and gesture recognition will be fully integrated, enabling intuitive control over every device and system. The home will no longer just be a place to live—it will be a responsive, adaptive environment that actively enhances comfort, productivity, and well-being.

Despite the undeniable benefits of AI's ubiquity, this profound integration of AI into personal, urban, and domestic life will bring significant challenges that must be addressed. One of the most pressing concerns is privacy. As AI systems gather and process unprecedented amounts of data—from health metrics and online activities to conversations and location tracking—questions around data ownership, consent, and security will grow increasingly urgent. Users will need assurances that their data is being handled transparently and ethically, without the risk of misuse or unauthorized access. Governments and companies will have to establish robust frameworks to protect individual privacy while enabling the functionality of AI systems.

Surveillance is another critical issue. The widespread deployment of AI-powered cameras and sensors in smart cities raises the specter of constant monitoring, potentially infringing on civil liberties. Predictive policing and facial recognition technologies, while effective in some contexts, risk reinforcing biases and disproportionately targeting certain communities if not carefully regulated. Strong governance frameworks will be essential to prevent misuse and ensure that these systems are designed and deployed with fairness, accountability, and transparency in mind.

Centralized control is another area of concern. As AI systems become integral to infrastructure, homes, and personal lives, the concentration of power in the hands of a few tech companies or governments could create vulnerabilities. Monopoly-like control over AI technologies could stifle competition, limit consumer choice, and increase dependency on a small number of providers. Moreover, centralized control creates a single point of failure. A cyberattack or system malfunction affecting an AI platform that powers critical infrastructure could disrupt entire cities or regions. Efforts to decentralize AI systems and build resilience into their design will be paramount.

The ubiquity of AI by 2030 will also blur the boundaries between human and machine interactions, raising philosophical and ethical questions about dependency and autonomy. As people grow increasingly reliant on AI for decision-making, there is a risk of diminishing critical thinking skills and individual agency. Over time, humans may come to trust AI systems implicitly, even in situations where skepticism or human judgment is essential. Balancing the convenience of AI with the preservation of human autonomy will require careful thought and proactive measures, including education and awareness campaigns about the limitations of AI.

The increasing presence of AI in everyday life will also create disparities between those who can access and afford advanced AI systems and those who cannot. While AI has the potential to reduce inequalities by making healthcare, education, and transportation more accessible, it could also deepen existing divides if its benefits are unevenly distributed.

Policymakers and companies will need to ensure that AI systems are designed inclusively, with affordability and accessibility at the forefront.

Despite these challenges, the ubiquity of AI by 2030 represents a tremendous opportunity to improve lives, enhance efficiency, and solve complex global challenges. With thoughtful planning, ethical design, and robust governance, AI can become a force for good, seamlessly integrating into every aspect of daily life while respecting individual rights and societal values. The world of 2030 will be one where AI is not just a tool but a partner, enriching human experiences and enabling progress on a scale previously unimaginable. The journey toward that future begins with the choices we make today, ensuring that AI's ubiquity serves the collective good rather than individual or institutional interests.

Chapter 25
The Evolving Workforce

By 2030, artificial intelligence (AI) will have fundamentally reshaped the global labor market. The changes won't simply involve automation replacing traditional jobs; instead, the workforce will evolve into a complex hybrid of human creativity and machine efficiency. New roles will emerge, traditional jobs will be transformed, and organizations will adapt to integrate AI into every aspect of their operations. While these advancements promise enormous potential, they also present challenges that demand thoughtful solutions. The future of work in an AI-driven world will be defined by collaboration, adaptability, and the ability to balance innovation with equity.

The most significant trend in the 2030 labor market will be the rise of hybrid work environments, where humans and AI collaborate seamlessly. Rather than replacing workers entirely, AI will complement human labor by automating repetitive, time-consuming tasks and enabling humans to focus on higher-value activities such as creativity, problem-solving, and emotional intelligence. For example, in healthcare, AI will handle administrative tasks like patient scheduling or insurance claims processing, allowing doctors and nurses to spend more time delivering personalized care. Similarly, in legal professions, AI will expedite contract analysis and legal research, leaving lawyers free to focus on strategy, negotiation, and client relationships.

Hybrid work environments will extend beyond individual roles to entire industries. Manufacturing, for example, will see human workers and AI-powered robotics working side by side on production lines, with machines handling precision tasks and humans overseeing quality control and troubleshooting. In education, teachers will collaborate with

AI tutors that adapt lesson plans to individual student needs, while in agriculture, farmers will use AI to monitor crops and predict yields, combining traditional skills with cutting-edge technology. The defining feature of hybrid work will be its ability to amplify human potential, enabling workers to achieve more and focus on tasks that require uniquely human qualities.

The gig economy, which has already transformed the labor market in the past decade, will enter a new phase by 2030, often referred to as "Gig Economy 2.0." AI-driven platforms will play a central role in connecting workers with opportunities, creating a more specialized and globalized gig ecosystem. Unlike the current gig economy, which is heavily reliant on low-skill, on-demand services like ride-sharing or food delivery, the next wave will facilitate specialized, high-skill gigs across industries. For example, a freelance data scientist in Brazil might use an AI platform to connect with a company in Japan seeking expertise in predictive analytics. Similarly, graphic designers, software developers, and even AI trainers will find work through global platforms that match their skills to specific projects.

This evolution of the gig economy will also include hyper-personalization. AI systems will analyze workers' skills, preferences, and work histories to recommend tailored opportunities, creating a more efficient and fulfilling labor market. Workers will have greater flexibility to choose projects that align with their interests and career goals, while employers will benefit from access to a global talent pool. However, this shift will also demand changes in labor policies, including protections for gig workers and mechanisms to ensure fair compensation in a highly competitive market.

The rise of AI will give birth to entirely new job categories, some of which may sound futuristic but will soon become commonplace. One of the most prominent roles will be that of the "AI ethicist," a professional responsible for ensuring that AI systems are designed and deployed in ways that align with ethical principles. AI ethicists will evaluate algorithms for fairness, transparency, and accountability, addressing biases and unintended consequences. Another emerging role will be that of the "human-AI collaboration designer," tasked with creating workflows and interfaces that optimize collaboration between humans and AI systems. These designers will focus on making AI tools intuitive and effective, ensuring that workers can harness their full potential.

The expansion of virtual and augmented reality technologies will also create demand for "virtual world architects," professionals who design and maintain immersive digital environments for purposes ranging from entertainment to education to remote work. These architects will combine technical skills with storytelling and user experience design, crafting virtual spaces that feel engaging and intuitive. Other new roles might include "AI trainers," who oversee the data used to train AI systems and ensure it meets quality standards, and "AI explainability specialists," who translate complex AI decisions into clear, actionable insights for non-technical stakeholders.

To adapt to the AI-integrated workplace, organizations will need to prioritize continuous upskilling and reskilling programs. The rapid pace of technological change will make lifelong learning a necessity for workers in all industries. Employers will invest in training programs that teach employees how to use AI tools effectively, as well as broader skills like critical thinking, creativity, and emotional intelligence that complement AI capabilities. For instance, a marketing professional might learn how to use AI-driven analytics platforms to identify trends in consumer behavior, while also developing storytelling skills to craft compelling campaigns.

AI-driven tools themselves will play a significant role in supporting workplace adaptation. These tools will enhance productivity by automating administrative tasks, such as scheduling meetings, managing emails, or generating reports. They will also provide actionable insights, helping workers make informed decisions more quickly. For example, an AI-powered dashboard might analyze sales data in real time, highlighting opportunities for growth or flagging potential risks. Collaboration tools will integrate AI to facilitate remote and hybrid work environments, automatically transcribing meetings, summarizing key points, and translating conversations across languages.

While the integration of AI into the workforce offers immense opportunities, it also presents challenges that must be addressed to ensure a fair and equitable transition. One of the most pressing concerns is income inequality. As AI automates certain tasks and displaces some jobs, the economic benefits of AI risk being concentrated among a small group of companies and highly skilled workers, leaving others behind. This growing divide could exacerbate social tensions and undermine trust in AI technologies. Policymakers and business leaders will need to take proactive measures to address these disparities, such as implementing progressive tax systems, ensuring fair wages, and redistributing the economic gains of AI through targeted investments in education and infrastructure.

Job displacement is another significant challenge. While AI will create new roles, it will also render some traditional jobs obsolete, particularly those involving routine, repetitive tasks. Workers in industries like manufacturing, retail, and transportation may face significant disruptions as automation reduces demand for their skills. To mitigate this impact, governments and organizations will need to invest heavily in reskilling initiatives, helping displaced workers transition into new roles. These programs should focus on teaching in-demand skills, such as data analysis, programming, and design, as well as soft skills that complement AI capabilities.

Social safety nets will play a critical role in supporting workers during this transition. Universal basic income (UBI) has been proposed as one potential solution, providing individuals with a guaranteed income regardless of employment status. While UBI remains a controversial policy, its proponents argue that it could provide financial security for workers displaced by AI, allowing them to pursue education, entrepreneurship, or other opportunities without the immediate pressure of finding a new job. Other measures, such as expanded unemployment benefits, subsidized childcare, and affordable healthcare, will also be essential to creating a more equitable labor market.

The evolving workforce will also raise questions about the nature of work itself. As AI takes over more routine tasks, humans will have the opportunity to focus on activities that are inherently creative, interpersonal, or purpose-driven. This shift could lead to a redefinition of success and fulfillment in the workplace, with greater emphasis on collaboration, innovation, and impact. However, it will also require a cultural shift, as workers and organizations learn to value these qualities over traditional measures of productivity.

Despite the challenges, the workforce of 2030 has the potential to be more dynamic, inclusive, and innovative than ever before. By embracing AI as a partner rather than a replacement, workers can achieve greater efficiency and creativity, while organizations can unlock new levels of performance and adaptability. The key to this transformation will be collaboration—between humans and machines, employers and employees, and governments and industries.

The labor market in 2030 will not simply be a continuation of the past; it will be a reimagining of what work means in a world where intelligence is no longer the sole domain of humans. With thoughtful planning, proactive policies, and a commitment to equity, the evolving workforce can become a powerful engine for progress, benefiting individuals, organizations, and societies as a whole. The challenges are significant, but so too are the opportunities to create a future of work that is not only efficient but also meaningful and inclusive.

Chapter 26
AI and the Global Economy

By 2030, artificial intelligence (AI) will be one of the most transformative forces in the global economy, reshaping industries, redefining trade, and driving unprecedented economic growth. AI's potential to enhance productivity, innovation, and efficiency is projected to contribute trillions of dollars to the global economy, making it a cornerstone of economic development. However, this transformation will not affect all nations or industries equally. While some countries and sectors will thrive, others risk being left behind, widening the gap between the AI leaders and those struggling to adapt. This chapter explores the economic potential of AI, the disparities it may exacerbate, the changes it will bring to global trade, and the challenges that must be addressed to create a more equitable and sustainable future.

AI is already proving to be a significant driver of economic growth, and by 2030, its impact will be even greater. Analysts project that AI could contribute as much as $15.7 trillion to the global economy by the end of the decade. This growth will be fueled by significant improvements in productivity as AI systems automate repetitive tasks, optimize processes, and uncover new efficiencies. For example, in manufacturing, AI-powered robotics will streamline production lines, reducing labor costs and increasing output. In retail, AI will enable personalized marketing and inventory optimization, driving higher sales and reducing waste. Across industries, AI will accelerate decision-making by providing real-time insights, allowing businesses to adapt more quickly to changing market conditions.

Innovation will also be a key driver of AI-driven economic growth. The technology will enable the creation of entirely new products, services, and business models, opening up previously untapped markets. In healthcare, for instance, AI will facilitate breakthroughs in drug discovery, enabling pharmaceutical companies to develop treatments faster and at lower costs. In the energy sector, AI will optimize the generation, storage, and distribution of renewable energy, making sustainable power more affordable and accessible. Financial services will benefit from AI's ability to detect fraud, assess credit risk, and automate complex transactions, creating a more efficient and secure global financial system. These innovations will not only boost corporate profits but also improve quality of life for billions of people.

Certain sectors will see particularly significant gains from AI adoption. Healthcare is expected to experience exponential growth as AI improves diagnostics, treatment, and care delivery. For example, AI-powered imaging tools will enable earlier detection of diseases like cancer, while predictive analytics will help hospitals manage resources more effectively. The finance industry will also be transformed, with AI-driven algorithms revolutionizing trading, lending, and risk management. Energy is another sector poised for disruption, as AI optimizes everything from grid management to the operation of wind turbines and solar panels. These advancements will not only drive economic growth but also help address critical global challenges such as access to healthcare and climate change.

While AI promises immense economic benefits, these gains will not be evenly distributed. Wealthier nations with advanced AI infrastructure and well-established technology ecosystems are likely to dominate the global economy, capturing the lion's share of AI-driven growth. Countries such as the United States, China, and members of the European Union are already investing heavily in AI research, development, and deployment. By 2030, these nations will likely consolidate their positions as global leaders in AI, leveraging their technological advantages to drive economic growth and secure geopolitical influence.

In contrast, many developing nations may struggle to keep pace. Limited access to data, computing power, and skilled talent will hinder their ability to adopt and benefit from AI technologies. This disparity risks creating a new form of digital divide, where the economic gains of AI are concentrated in a few wealthy nations while others are left behind. For example, countries with insufficient infrastructure may find it difficult to deploy AI in critical areas such as agriculture, healthcare, and education, exacerbating existing inequalities and limiting their ability to compete in the global economy.

Bridging this divide will require concerted international collaboration, knowledge-sharing, and investment. Wealthier nations and multinational organizations must play a role in democratizing access to AI technologies and expertise. Initiatives such as open-source AI models, cross-border research partnerships, and educational programs can help level the playing field. For instance, international organizations like the United Nations and the World Bank could fund projects to improve AI infrastructure in developing countries, enabling them to participate in the AI economy. Similarly, universities and private companies could offer training programs to build AI expertise in underserved regions, fostering local innovation and talent development.

AI will also revolutionize global trade, creating more efficient and resilient supply chains. Predictive analytics will enable companies to forecast demand more accurately, reducing overproduction and waste. Real-time optimization will allow businesses to adjust supply chain operations dynamically, responding to changes in demand, weather conditions, or geopolitical events. For instance, an AI system might reroute shipments to avoid delays caused by natural disasters or political unrest, ensuring timely delivery of goods.

Logistics will be transformed by autonomous vehicles and drones, which will redefine how goods are transported and delivered. Self-driving trucks will reduce transportation costs by minimizing labor expenses and fuel consumption, while drones will enable faster and more flexible last-mile deliveries. These advancements will make global trade networks more reliable and cost-effective, benefiting both businesses and consumers. AI will also facilitate cross-border e-commerce by automating customs processes, translating product descriptions, and tailoring marketing strategies for different markets, further integrating the global economy.

However, the integration of AI into global trade and the broader economy will also present challenges. One of the most significant concerns is the concentration of economic power in a small number of AI-dominant corporations and nations. Tech giants such as Google, Amazon, Alibaba, and Tencent are already leveraging their AI capabilities to gain a competitive edge in multiple industries, from retail and advertising to cloud computing and logistics. By 2030, these companies could wield even greater influence, potentially stifling competition and innovation. Similarly, nations that lead in AI development may use their technological advantages to assert economic and geopolitical dominance, exacerbating global inequalities.

Addressing these challenges will require new trade policies and regulatory frameworks that promote fairness and inclusivity. Governments must ensure that AI-driven innovation does not result in monopolistic practices or exploitative behaviors. For example, antitrust regulations could be updated to address the unique dynamics of AI markets, preventing dominant players from using their technological advantages to suppress competition. Trade agreements could include provisions to ensure that the benefits of AI are shared more equitably, such as by requiring technology transfer or capacity-building initiatives in developing countries.

Another challenge is the potential for job displacement as AI automates tasks across industries. While AI will create new economic opportunities, it will also disrupt traditional employment patterns, potentially leading to significant job losses in sectors such as manufacturing, transportation, and customer service. Policymakers will need to implement strategies to mitigate these impacts, such as investing in education and reskilling programs to prepare workers for the jobs of the future. Social safety nets, including unemployment benefits and universal basic income, may also play a role in supporting individuals affected by economic transitions.

Despite these challenges, the integration of AI into the global economy offers enormous potential for progress. By harnessing AI's capabilities, businesses can achieve greater efficiency and innovation, governments can address critical societal challenges, and individuals can benefit from improved goods, services, and opportunities. The key to realizing this potential will be ensuring that the benefits of AI are distributed equitably, both within and between nations. Collaboration, regulation, and inclusive policies will be essential to creating a global economy that is not only more productive but also more just and sustainable.

By 2030, the global economy will have been fundamentally transformed by AI. The technology will drive trillions of dollars in economic growth, revolutionize industries, and redefine global trade. However, realizing the full potential of AI will require overcoming significant challenges, including economic disparities, monopolistic practices, and job displacement. With thoughtful planning and collective action, AI can become a powerful engine for economic progress, benefiting people and nations around the world. The choices made today will shape the trajectory of AI in the coming decade, determining whether it serves as a tool for shared prosperity or a driver of inequality.

Chapter 27
Ethics and Governance in 2030

As artificial intelligence (AI) becomes an integral part of everyday life by 2030, ethical considerations and governance frameworks will take center stage in shaping its role in society. The rapid adoption of AI across industries and borders has the potential to deliver transformative benefits, but it also introduces risks that could undermine privacy, equality, and human rights. Navigating these challenges will require the development of robust ethical standards and governance systems that ensure AI serves humanity responsibly and equitably. This chapter explores the state of global AI governance in 2030, the importance of safeguarding human rights in an AI-driven world, the measures needed to build public trust, and the challenges that come with balancing innovation and regulation.

By 2030, AI governance will have evolved into a global endeavor, with international coalitions playing a central role in regulating the development and deployment of AI technologies. Much like agreements on climate change or nuclear weapons, standardized regulations for AI will likely emerge as a necessity to address shared risks and promote ethical practices across borders. These frameworks will establish guidelines for transparency, accountability, and fairness, ensuring that AI systems are not only effective but also aligned with societal values.

International agreements on AI governance will include mechanisms for auditing and certifying AI systems to ensure compliance with ethical standards. For instance, organizations deploying AI in critical areas such as healthcare, finance, or law enforcement may be required to undergo regular audits to verify that their systems are free from bias, operate transparently, and produce equitable outcomes. Non-compliance with these regulations could result in penalties, such as fines or restrictions on the use of AI technologies. These enforcement measures will encourage organizations to prioritize ethical considerations in the design and deployment of their AI systems.

Global governance frameworks will also address the risks associated with the misuse of AI, such as the development of autonomous weapons or the manipulation of public opinion through deepfakes and misinformation. Nations will collaborate to establish treaties that prohibit harmful applications of AI, much like existing agreements on chemical and biological weapons. These treaties will include provisions for monitoring and enforcement, ensuring that countries adhere to their commitments and that violations are addressed swiftly and effectively.

The ethical use of AI will also require a strong focus on safeguarding human rights, particularly as AI systems become more deeply embedded in areas such as surveillance, the justice system, and employment. By 2030, the protection of privacy, autonomy, and freedom from AI-driven discrimination will remain key priorities for governments, organizations, and civil society. AI technologies that process personal data will need to comply with stringent privacy regulations, ensuring that individuals retain control over their information and are not subjected to unwarranted surveillance or data exploitation.

In the justice system, AI will play a significant role in areas such as sentencing, parole decisions, and crime prevention. However, the potential for bias in AI algorithms poses a serious threat to fairness and equality. For example, systems trained on historical data may inadvertently reinforce existing racial or socioeconomic disparities, leading to discriminatory outcomes. To address this, governments will establish oversight mechanisms to ensure that AI systems in the justice sector are transparent, unbiased, and accountable. Independent review boards may be tasked with auditing these systems and providing recommendations for improvement.

In the realm of employment, AI-driven hiring platforms and workplace monitoring tools will need to respect workers' rights and avoid discriminatory practices. For instance, algorithms used to screen job applicants must be designed to evaluate candidates equitably, without favoring or excluding individuals based on factors such as gender, race, or age. Governments and organizations will need to implement safeguards to ensure that AI systems promote inclusivity and diversity in the workplace.

Building public trust in AI technologies will be critical to their widespread adoption and acceptance. By 2030, transparency will be a fundamental requirement for AI systems, ensuring that individuals understand how algorithms make decisions and how those decisions impact their lives. Organizations will be expected to provide clear, accessible explanations of their AI systems' operations, including the data used for training, the logic behind decision-making processes, and the limitations of their technologies.

Active public engagement will also play a vital role in fostering trust. Citizen oversight boards and participatory governance models may emerge as mechanisms for giving individuals a voice in how AI is developed and deployed. These boards could include representatives from diverse communities, ensuring that the perspectives of marginalized or underrepresented groups are considered in decision-making processes. For example, a citizen oversight board might review the use of AI in urban planning, ensuring that smart city initiatives prioritize inclusivity and do not disproportionately benefit affluent neighborhoods at the expense of others.

Educational initiatives will further enhance public trust by demystifying AI and empowering individuals to make informed decisions about its use. Schools, universities, and community organizations will offer programs on AI literacy, teaching people how to engage with AI systems responsibly and critically. Public awareness campaigns will also highlight the benefits and risks of AI, promoting a balanced understanding of its potential.

Despite these efforts, achieving a balance between innovation and regulation will remain one of the most significant challenges in AI governance. On one hand, excessive regulation could stifle technological progress, limiting the potential benefits of AI and hindering its ability to address complex global challenges. On the other hand, insufficient regulation could allow harmful or unethical practices to proliferate, undermining public trust and exacerbating social inequalities.

Striking this balance will require careful negotiation between governments, businesses, and civil society. Policymakers will need to craft regulations that are flexible enough to accommodate new developments in AI while still providing robust protections for individuals and communities. For example, adaptive regulatory frameworks that evolve alongside technological advancements could help address emerging risks without hindering innovation. These frameworks might include "sandbox" environments where companies can test new AI applications under regulatory supervision, allowing for experimentation while minimizing potential harms.

The role of private companies in AI governance will also be critical. By 2030, many of the world's leading AI innovations will continue to come from the private sector, placing significant responsibility on corporations to act ethically and transparently. Companies will need to adopt internal governance frameworks that align with global standards, including ethical guidelines for AI development and deployment. For instance, organizations might establish ethics committees or appoint chief AI ethics officers to oversee the responsible use of AI technologies.

Collaboration between the public and private sectors will be essential to addressing shared challenges and ensuring that AI serves the collective good. Governments and companies will need to work together to develop standards for data sharing, algorithmic accountability, and system interoperability. Public-private partnerships could also play a role in advancing research on ethical AI, funding initiatives that explore new ways to mitigate bias, enhance transparency, and improve user understanding.

The challenges of governing AI in 2030 will extend beyond technical and regulatory considerations to include broader societal and philosophical questions. As AI systems become more autonomous and capable, questions about accountability, agency, and moral responsibility will become increasingly complex. For example, if an autonomous vehicle causes an accident, who should be held responsible—the manufacturer, the software developer, or the owner? Similarly, as AI systems take on roles traditionally performed by humans, such as caregiving or decision-making, society will need to grapple with questions about the ethical implications of delegating these responsibilities to machines.

The ethical and governance challenges posed by AI will also intersect with broader issues of global inequality and power dynamics. For instance, the concentration of AI expertise and resources in a few wealthy nations and corporations could exacerbate global disparities, leaving developing countries at a disadvantage. Addressing these inequalities will require international cooperation and a commitment to ensuring that the benefits of AI are distributed equitably. This might involve initiatives to build AI capacity in under-resourced regions, such as funding for education, infrastructure, and research.

Looking ahead to 2030, ethics and governance will be the foundation upon which the future of AI is built. By establishing robust frameworks for regulation, transparency, and accountability, society can ensure that AI technologies are developed and deployed in ways that respect human rights, promote public trust, and balance innovation with societal values. The decisions made today will shape the trajectory of AI for decades to come, determining whether it becomes a force for progress and equity or a source of division and harm. With thoughtful planning, proactive collaboration, and a commitment to ethical principles, the world can harness the transformative potential of AI while safeguarding the interests of all humanity.

Chapter 28
AI and the Human Experience

By 2030, artificial intelligence (AI) will not merely be a transformative force for industries and economies—it will fundamentally reshape the human experience itself. The integration of AI into daily life will redefine relationships, augment creativity and intelligence, and challenge humanity to reconsider the meaning of purpose and fulfillment in a world where machines can perform many traditional tasks. As AI becomes an intrinsic part of existence, it will create opportunities for profound growth and connection but will also introduce ethical dilemmas and societal challenges. The choices made today in designing and deploying AI will determine whether it enhances or diminishes what it means to be human.

Redefining Relationships

AI will revolutionize the way humans connect and interact, both with each other and with machines. By 2030, AI-powered companions will become commonplace, offering individuals new forms of interaction, intimacy, and emotional support. These companions will be capable of mimicking human-like conversations, understanding emotions, and providing personalized feedback. For some, they will become confidants, helping alleviate loneliness and offering guidance during difficult times. AI companions may be particularly valuable for the elderly, who often experience isolation, or for individuals with disabilities, offering assistance and companionship tailored to their specific needs.

Virtual worlds, enhanced by AI, will also play a significant role in redefining relationships. Immersive environments powered by AI will allow people to connect in ways that transcend physical boundaries, enabling interactions that feel as real as face-to-face encounters. Virtual meetings, social events, and even romantic relationships will increasingly take place in these AI-driven spaces, blurring the lines between physical and digital realities. These environments will be dynamic, adapting to the preferences and emotions of their users, creating shared experiences that feel deeply personal and meaningful.

However, the rise of human-AI relationships will spark ethical debates about authenticity, autonomy, and emotional well-being. Can a relationship with an AI companion be as meaningful as one with a human? Will relying on AI for emotional support undermine the development of genuine human connections? These questions will challenge society to reconsider the essence of relationships and the boundaries of intimacy. Concerns about dependency on AI companions may also arise, particularly if individuals begin to prioritize interactions with machines over those with other humans. Safeguards will be needed to ensure that AI complements, rather than replaces, human relationships.

Augmented Creativity and Intelligence

One of AI's most profound impacts on the human experience will be its ability to amplify creativity and intelligence. By 2030, AI systems will collaborate with humans to produce art, music, literature, and other forms of creative expression. These systems will generate ideas, explore stylistic possibilities, and even create complete works, while humans provide direction, emotional resonance, and final refinement. For example, an AI might compose a symphony based on a user's emotional input, with the human artist adding their unique touch to make the composition truly their own.

AI will also democratize creativity, enabling individuals without formal training or expertise to produce professional-quality work. A person with no background in painting, for instance, could use AI tools to create stunning visual art by describing their vision or selecting elements from a digital palette. Similarly, writers will be able to collaborate with AI to overcome writer's block, generate compelling narratives, or explore alternative storylines. This partnership between human creativity and machine intelligence will unlock new avenues for self-expression and innovation, enriching cultural and artistic landscapes.

Advancements in brain-computer interfaces (BCIs) will further expand the possibilities for human-AI collaboration. By enabling direct communication between human thought and AI systems, BCIs will allow individuals to harness the cognitive power of AI in real time. Imagine a scientist brainstorming solutions to a complex problem with the assistance of an AI system that can instantly analyze vast amounts of data and suggest potential approaches. Or consider an artist who can visualize an idea in their mind and see it materialize on a digital canvas through their neural connection to an AI-powered design tool. These interfaces will not only enhance human capabilities but also challenge traditional notions of intelligence and creativity, as the boundaries between human and machine blur.

While the potential of augmented creativity and intelligence is immense, it also raises questions about originality, authenticity, and the role of the artist or thinker. If an AI system contributes significantly to the creation of a work, who should receive credit? How will society value human effort in a world where machines can produce masterpieces? These questions will require new frameworks for defining and rewarding creativity in an AI-driven era.

The Role of Purpose

As AI automates more tasks and reduces the need for human labor in many areas, individuals will be freed from routine, repetitive work. This shift will prompt a reevaluation of purpose and fulfillment, as people seek to redefine their roles in a world where traditional notions of productivity and achievement are no longer the primary measures of success. By 2030, societal values around work, leisure, and accomplishment will have evolved significantly, reflecting the opportunities and challenges presented by AI.

For many, the automation of labor will open up new possibilities for creativity, exploration, and social connection. Freed from the constraints of traditional employment, individuals may devote more time to pursuing passions, learning new skills, or engaging with their communities. For example, a person who no longer needs to work a nine-to-five job might spend their time volunteering, traveling, or pursuing artistic endeavors. This shift could lead to a more fulfilling and balanced way of life, where meaning is derived from personal growth and relationships rather than economic productivity.

Societies will also need to grapple with questions about the distribution of wealth and resources in a world where AI drives economic growth. Universal basic income (UBI) and other social safety nets may play a critical role in ensuring that individuals have the financial security to explore new sources of purpose. Education systems will need to adapt, emphasizing creativity, critical thinking, and emotional intelligence over rote memorization and technical skills that can be automated. Governments, organizations, and communities will need to foster environments that support lifelong learning and personal development, enabling individuals to thrive in an AI-driven world.

However, the shift away from traditional labor will also pose challenges. For some, the loss of work as a central source of identity and purpose may lead to feelings of alienation or aimlessness. Societies will need to address these psychological and cultural shifts, ensuring that individuals can find meaning and connection in other ways. This may involve reimagining social structures, creating new rituals and traditions, or fostering a greater sense of community and shared responsibility.

Challenges

While the integration of AI into the human experience holds immense promise, it also presents significant challenges that must be addressed to ensure it enhances, rather than diminishes, what it means to be human. One of the most pressing concerns is the ethical design of AI systems. Developers and policymakers will need to prioritize transparency, accountability, and fairness, ensuring that AI technologies align with human values and do not perpetuate harm or inequality. For example, AI systems used in healthcare or education must be designed to prioritize patient and student needs, rather than maximizing profits or reinforcing biases.

The potential for dependency on AI also raises concerns. As individuals come to rely on AI for emotional support, creativity, and decision-making, there is a risk that human autonomy and agency may be diminished. Safeguards will be needed to ensure that AI serves as a tool for empowerment, rather than a substitute for human effort and judgment. For example, AI companions should be designed to encourage real-world connections and social interactions, rather than isolating users in virtual relationships.

The rise of virtual worlds and augmented realities will also pose challenges related to identity, authenticity, and mental health. As individuals spend more time in AI-driven environments, questions about the nature of reality and the impact of digital experiences on well-being will become increasingly important. Societies will need to establish guidelines and support systems to ensure that virtual experiences enhance, rather than detract from, individuals' overall quality of life.

Final Thoughts

By 2030, AI will be deeply woven into the fabric of human life, reshaping not only industries and economies but also the very essence of what it means to be human. It will redefine relationships, augment creativity and intelligence, and challenge individuals and societies to reconsider their values, priorities, and sources of meaning. While the future holds immense promise, it also brings significant challenges that must be addressed through innovation, governance, and collective action.

The integration of AI into the human experience will require careful thought and ethical foresight. Developers, policymakers, and communities will need to work together to ensure that AI technologies enhance human potential while safeguarding autonomy, authenticity, and well-being. The choices made today will define the role of AI in shaping the world of tomorrow, determining whether it becomes a force for connection, creativity, and purpose—or a source of division, dependency, and alienation.

As humanity navigates this transformation, one thing is clear: the relationship between humans and AI will be one of the defining narratives of the 21st century. By embracing the opportunities and addressing the challenges, we can create a future where AI enriches the human experience, enabling individuals and societies to thrive in ways that were once unimaginable.

Conclusion: The Human-AI Odyssey

As we stand on the threshold of 2030, artificial intelligence (AI) has emerged as a transformative force, reshaping every aspect of human life, from industries and economies to relationships and individual purpose. Over the past decade, AI has evolved from a specialized tool into a ubiquitous presence, seamlessly integrated into the fabric of daily existence. Its profound impact is felt across global economies, personal lives, and the societal structures that define our shared humanity. Yet, as the promise of AI unfolds, it brings with it a host of challenges, uncertainties, and ethical dilemmas that will shape the trajectory of the future.

The journey of AI development is not merely a technical endeavour—it is a human one. The choices made in governance, ethics, and design will determine whether AI fulfils its potential as a force for progress and equity or exacerbates divisions and inequalities. As AI grows more intelligent, autonomous, and pervasive, humanity must ensure that it remains a tool of empowerment rather than domination, a partner in human progress rather than a source of alienation.

The Transformative Power of AI

AI's influence by 2030 will span nearly every domain of human activity, driving unprecedented innovation, efficiency, and creativity. It will revolutionize industries such as healthcare, education, energy, and transportation, unlocking solutions to some of the world's most pressing challenges. In healthcare, AI will save lives by enabling earlier diagnoses, personalized treatments, and predictive care. In education, it will democratize access to knowledge, providing tailored learning experiences to individuals across the globe. Renewable energy systems will be optimized by AI, accelerating the transition to sustainability, while autonomous vehicles and drones will redefine mobility and logistics.

AI will not only transform existing systems but also create entirely new possibilities. It will amplify human creativity by collaborating with artists, writers, and musicians, generating ideas and works that were previously unimaginable. Brain-computer interfaces will blur the boundaries between thought and technology, enabling direct collaboration between human cognition and AI systems. Virtual worlds powered by AI will allow for richer, more immersive experiences, reshaping how people interact, work, and play.

The economic impact of AI will also be staggering. By automating tasks, optimizing processes, and uncovering new efficiencies, AI is projected to contribute trillions of dollars to the global economy. It will drive innovation, create new industries, and redefine the nature of work. However, the benefits of AI will not be evenly distributed, and addressing this disparity will be one of the great challenges of the AI era.

The Ethical Imperative

As AI becomes more powerful, the ethical considerations surrounding its development and deployment will grow more urgent. The potential for harm—from biased algorithms to invasive surveillance—underscores the need for robust governance frameworks and ethical guidelines. By 2030, the world will need global coalitions to regulate AI, ensuring that it aligns with shared values such as transparency, accountability, and fairness.

AI's integration into areas like justice, hiring, and healthcare raises critical questions about human rights. Can we ensure that AI-driven systems do not perpetuate discrimination or inequality? How do we safeguard privacy and autonomy in a world where AI systems process vast amounts of personal data? These questions will require thoughtful, proactive solutions that balance innovation with the protection of individual freedoms.

Public trust in AI will be essential to its adoption and success. Transparent systems, active public engagement, and participatory governance models will be critical for building this trust. Citizen oversight boards, AI audits, and educational initiatives will empower individuals to understand and shape the role of AI in their lives. By fostering a culture of accountability and inclusivity, society can ensure that AI serves as a force for good rather than a source of division.

The Human Experience in an AI World

Perhaps the most profound impact of AI will be on the human experience itself. By automating routine tasks, AI will free individuals to focus on creativity, exploration, and connection. It will challenge traditional notions of work, purpose, and achievement, prompting societies to reconsider what it means to live a meaningful life.

AI companions and virtual worlds will redefine relationships, offering new forms of intimacy and interaction. While these innovations hold promise, they also raise ethical and philosophical questions about authenticity and emotional well-being. As humans form bonds with AI systems, society will need to navigate the complexities of these relationships, ensuring that they complement rather than replace human connections.

At the same time, AI's ability to augment creativity and intelligence will unlock unprecedented potential. By collaborating with AI systems, individuals will achieve feats of innovation and expression that transcend the limits of human capability. This partnership between humans and machines will redefine the boundaries of creativity, intelligence, and art, enriching cultural and intellectual landscapes.

The rise of AI will also prompt a reevaluation of societal values. As work becomes less central to human identity, individuals may seek new sources of purpose in creativity, community, and personal growth. Education systems will need to emphasize emotional intelligence, critical thinking, and adaptability, preparing individuals for a world where traditional skills are no longer the primary measure of success.

Challenges and Responsibilities

While the promise of AI is immense, the challenges it presents are equally significant. The concentration of power in a few AI-dominant corporations and nations risks exacerbating global inequalities, creating a divide between those who benefit from AI and those who are left behind. Bridging this gap will require international collaboration, investments in AI infrastructure, and efforts to democratize access to AI technologies.

Job displacement is another pressing concern. While AI will create new roles and industries, it will also render some traditional jobs obsolete. Governments, organizations, and communities will need to invest in reskilling programs, social safety nets, and policies that ensure economic security for all. Universal basic income, expanded unemployment benefits, and affordable education may play critical roles in supporting individuals during this transition.

The ethical dilemmas surrounding AI will also require ongoing attention. As AI becomes more autonomous, questions about accountability, agency, and moral responsibility will become increasingly complex. Who should be held responsible for the actions of an AI system? How do we ensure that AI aligns with human values? These questions will require new legal, philosophical, and practical frameworks.

A Shared Responsibility

The future of AI is not predetermined. It will be shaped by the decisions and actions of governments, businesses, researchers, and individuals. Ensuring that AI enhances the human experience will require a shared commitment to ethical design, equitable access, and inclusive governance. Collaboration across sectors and borders will be essential to addressing the challenges and unlocking the opportunities of the AI era.

Researchers and developers must prioritize transparency, accountability, and fairness in their work, ensuring that AI systems are designed to serve humanity. Policymakers must craft regulations that balance innovation with societal values, protecting human rights while fostering technological progress. Businesses must act responsibly, adopting ethical practices and investing in the well-being of their workers and communities.

Individuals, too, have a role to play. By engaging with AI technologies critically and thoughtfully, citizens can shape the direction of AI development and ensure that it reflects their values and priorities. Education and awareness will be key to empowering individuals to navigate the complexities of an AI-driven world.

Final Thoughts: A Human-AI Partnership

As we look toward 2030 and beyond, AI offers humanity a unique opportunity to reimagine what is possible. It has the potential to solve problems that have long seemed insurmountable, from curing diseases to combating climate change. It can enrich lives through creativity, connection, and exploration, enabling individuals to achieve their full potential. But realizing this vision will require humanity to rise to the challenges of the AI era, ensuring that this powerful technology is guided by wisdom, compassion, and a commitment to the common good.

The story of AI is ultimately the story of humanity—of our creativity, ambition, and resilience. It is a story of how we choose to use the tools we create, and what we value as a species. By embracing the possibilities of AI while addressing its risks, we can build a future where technology serves humanity's highest aspirations, enriching lives and creating a more just, inclusive, and sustainable world.

In the end, the true measure of AI's success will not be its intelligence or capabilities, but its ability to enhance the human spirit and elevate the human experience. The choices we make today will define the legacy of AI for generations to come, forging a partnership between humans and machines that reflects the best of who we are and who we aspire to become.